DK EYEWITNESS

T0104262

TOP10
VIENNA

Top 10 Vienna Highlights

The Top 10 of Everything

CONTENTS

Vienna
Area by Area

Streetsmart

Within each Top 10 list in this book, no hierarchy of quality or popularity is implied. All 10 are, in the editor's opinion, of roughly equal merit.

Title page, front cover and spine *Magnificent interior of the Jesuit Church, Vienna*
Back cover, clockwise from top left *The sprawling Stadt park; Gloriette in Schönbrunn Palace; aerial view of Rosshelen; the Jesuit Church; the vibrant Hundertwasser house*

The rapid rate at which the world is changing is constantly keeping the DK Eyewitness team on our toes. While we've worked hard to ensure that this edition of Vienna is accurate and up-to-date, we know that opening hours alter, standards shift, prices fluctuate, places close and new ones pop up in their stead. So, if you notice we've got something wrong or left something out, we want to hear about it. Please get in touch at **travelguides@dk.com**

Welcome to
Vienna

Bold, Baroque and achingly beautiful, Vienna's storied streets owe much to the extravagant creative splurges of Empress Maria Theresa and Emperor Franz Joseph during the time of the Austro-Hungarian Empire. From the opulent façades on Ringstrasse to the imperial grandeur of Schloss Schönbrunn, Vienna epitomizes decadence in all its glory. With DK Eyewitness Top 10 Vienna, it is yours to explore.

Vienna is home to the Gothic spires of **Stephansdom** and the Prater's iconic **Giant Ferris Wheel** as well as the world-famous Lipizzaner horses of the **Spanish Riding School**. An enviable array of galleries and museums rub shoulders with a plethora of cultural venues that draw visitors from all over the world. Holding court in the midst of it all is the sprawling **Hofburg** palace: the imposing royal seat of the Habsburg dynasty for over six centuries, with its fascinating heritage, gilded decor and sumptuous art.

Contemporary museums and cutting-edge architecture generate a modern buzz in this historical city, creating a pleasing juxtaposition of old and new. The city and its shimmering ballrooms have long been synonymous with the super-charged Viennese Waltz. Yet, in Vienna's idiosyncratic districts, you'll find a beguiling mishmash of hip streets and faded grandeur together with the oils, spices and food stalls of the famous **Naschmarkt**.

Whether you're visiting for a weekend or a week, our Top 10 guide brings together the best of everything the city has to offer, from a rich pedigree in classical music to *Kaffeehaus* culture. The guide has useful tips throughout, from seeking out what's free to getting off the beaten track, plus eight easy-to-follow itineraries, designed to tie together a clutch of sights in a short space of time. Add inspiring photography and detailed maps, and you've got the essential pocket-sized travel companion. **Enjoy the book, and enjoy Vienna.**

Clockwise from top: **Façade of the Burgtheater, Johann Strauss Monument, patterned roof of Stephansdom, the majestic Upper Belvedere, Ferris wheel in the Prater, interior of Café Central, exterior of the Majolika Haus**

Exploring Vienna

Vienna's compact centre, with its jaw-dropping high culture and dazzling Habsburg-era palaces, is easily walkable. Visitors can explore its wonderful maze of backstreets that twist and turn past historic cafés and fascinating museums alike.

Vienna's Spanish Riding School, with its Lipizzaner stallions, is world famous.

Two Days in Vienna

Day ❶
MORNING
Start at the imperial **Hofburg** palace (see pp16–21) with a coffee under gilded chandeliers at **Café Hofburg** (see p98). Delve into the lives of the Habsburg monarchs at the Sisi Museum before visiting the world-renowned **Spanish Riding School** (see pp20–21). Pass the **Albertina** museum (see p91), with its wide-ranging collections of art, before indulging yourself with a gourmet Austrian lunch at **Restaurant im Hotel Ambassador** (see p78).

AFTERNOON
Head to the **Staatsoper** (see pp36–7) for a fascinating backstage tour. Then to the **Hotel Sacher** (see p142) for a slice of Sachertorte (chocolate cake) at a table with a view of the street – it's a perfect people-watching spot.

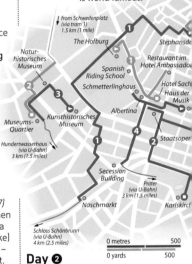

from Schwedenplatz (via tram 1) 1.5 km (1 mile)

The Hofburg

Stephansd.

Naturhistorisches Museum

Spanish Riding School

Schmetterlinghaus

Restaurant im Hotel Ambassado.

Hotel Sach. Haus der Musik

Albertina

Museums-Quartier

Kunsthistorisches Museum

Staatsoper

Hundertwasserhaus (via U-Bahn) 3 km (1.5 miles)

Secession Building

Prater (via U-Bahn) 3 km (1.5 miles)

Naschmarkt

Karlskirch.

Schloss Schönbrunn (via U-Bahn) 4 km (2.5 miles)

| 0 metres | 500 |
| 0 yards | 500 |

Day ❷
MORNING
Climb the 137-m (450-ft) South Tower of the elaborately tiled **Stephansdom** (see pp12–15) for mesmerizing views of the city. Afterwards, grab a kerbside table at **Café Diglas** (see p98) on Fleischmarkt to enjoy an *Einspänner* (cream-topped coffee) and a bite to eat overlooking the crowds.

AFTERNOON
To sightsee in vintage style, hop aboard tram 1 at Schwedenplatz to trundle around the Ringstrasse boulevard. Spend the rest of the day at the **MuseumsQuartier** (see pp34–5) in Museumsplatz. In addition to the wealth of museums to dip into, the courtyards host dance, film festivals, recitals and DJs in fine weather.

The Staatsoper, Vienna's State Opera House, has an elegant interior.

Greater Vienna

Area of main map

Prater

Hundertwasser-haus

Schloss Schönbrunn

0 km   2
0 miles   2

Key
━ Two-day itinerary
━ Four-day itinerary

MuseumsQuartier
(via tram 1)
3.5 km (2 miles)

Schwedenplatz

Café Diglas

Stadtpark

The Belvedere

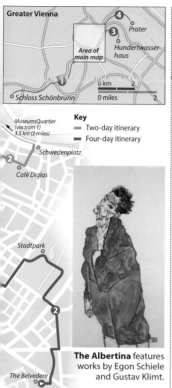

The Albertina features works by Egon Schiele and Gustav Klimt.

Kunsthistorisches Museum's opulent galleries treat art lovers to a visual feast.

the fragrant gardens before a visit to the 6.5-ha (16-acre) **Stadtpark** (see p64) to see its beautiful sculptures.

AFTERNOON

At the **Albertina** (see p91) you'll find paintings, a million graphic works and thousands of early photographs. Enjoy a backstage tour at the grand **Staatsoper** (see pp36–7) before a visit to **Karlskirche** (see pp32–3).

Day ❸

MORNING

After marvelling at the magnificent collections of the **Kunsthistorisches Museum** (see pp22–5), delve into the artifacts at the **Naturhistorisches Museum** (see p107).

AFTERNOON

Stop at the Leopold Museum in the **MuseumsQuartier** (see pp34–5) to see the works of Gustav Klimt, and then head to the **Hundertwasserhaus** (see pp40–41), a colourful modern building designed by Friedensreich Hundertwasser.

Day ❹

MORNING

Enjoy fun-filled family interaction at the **Haus der Musik** (see p57) before a visit to the **Schmetterlinghaus** (see p69), home to hundreds of butterflies in a colourful tropical setting.

AFTERNOON

Pay a visit to the 1897 **Secession Building** (see pp38–9), once home to a breakaway group of artists led by Gustav Klimt. Round off the day exploring the **Prater** (see p64) – a former royal hunting ground with a famous Ferris wheel.

Four Days in Vienna

Day ❶

MORNING

Browse **Stephansdom** (see pp12–15) before exploring the grandeur of the **Hofburg** palace (see pp16–21) and 450 years of tradition at the **Spanish Riding School** (see pp20–21).

AFTERNOON

Meander through the food stalls of the **Naschmarkt** (see p116), piled high with produce. Next, head to **Schloss Schönbrunn** (see pp42–5), the royal summer residence, for its Rococo rooms, fountains and gardens.

Day ❷

MORNING

Take time to stroll around the lovely **Belvedere** (see pp28–31) and admire

Top 10 Vienna Highlights

**Detail of sculptural decoration on
the exterior of the Hofburg**

🔟 Vienna Highlights

Packed with splendid edifices, grand palaces and imposing churches that span the centuries, Vienna oozes charm and atmosphere. The city's imperial grandeur can still be felt, yet there's much more on offer here, including stunning museums, a vibrant café culture and lively nightclubs.

1 Stephansdom

The Gothic cathedral is one of the city's most prominent landmarks. From its spire you can enjoy spectacular views over the rooftops *(see pp12–15).*

2 The Hofburg

The old imperial palace, with its many wings and courtyards and stunning interior, reflects Austria's glorious past. It is still the setting for grand balls *(see pp16–21).*

3 Kunsthistorisches Museum

This remarkable museum contains one of the world's largest collections of Old Masters *(see pp22–5).*

4 The Belvedere

The former summer residence of the 17th-century war hero Prince Eugene is a splendid Baroque palace that is now home to the Austrian Gallery. It houses Gustav Klimt's *The Kiss (see pp28–31).*

⑤ Karlskirche
This impressive Baroque church has a column on either side and a large dome overhead. It is a fine sight dominating Karlsplatz *(see pp32–3)*.

⑥ MuseumsQuartier
The former imperial stables have been converted into a large museum complex exhibiting, among other things, collections of contemporary and modern art *(see pp34–5)*.

⑦ Staatsoper
The Vienna State Opera attracts music lovers from all over the world. Its grand auditorium is a fitting introduction to an evening of classical music *(see pp36–7)*.

⑧ Secession Building
The simple white Secession Building is a magnificent Art Nouveau edifice that reflects the ideals of the Secessionist movement – purity and functionalism *(see pp38–9)*.

⑨ Hundertwasserhaus
Designed by Austrian artist Friedensreich Hundertwasser, this unconventional building is famous for its uneven floors, rooftop gardens and unique windows *(see pp40–41)*.

⑩ Schloss Schönbrunn
The former summer home of the imperial Habsburg family remains a magnificent palace, with splendid Baroque gardens and the world's oldest zoo *(see pp42–5)*.

⬛🔟⭐ Stephansdom

Located in the heart of the city, St Stephen's Cathedral is Vienna's most beloved landmark and Austria's finest Gothic edifice. The foundations of the original Romanesque church date back to 1147, but the earliest surviving features today are the 13th-century Giant's Door and the Heathen Towers on the west front. Various Habsburg rulers left their imprints by rebuilding the Gothic nave, the side chapels and the choir in the 14th and 15th centuries. The "Steffl", as the cathedral is called by the Viennese, suffered damage from World War II bombings, but its rebuilding was a symbol of hope as the country emerged from the ashes of the conflict.

③ Tiled Roof
The impressive roof **(left)** is covered with almost 230,000 colourful tiles laid out in the form of the Habsburg coat of arms, depicting a double-headed eagle wearing the emperor's crown and the Golden Fleece. Originally built before 1474, the roof was restored after fire damage in World War II.

④ Giant's Door
After a mammoth's bone was found on the site during 15th-century construction works, the cathedral's main gate was renamed. It is decorated with sculptures that show Christ on Judgement Day between two angels.

① Windows
The five medieval stained-glass windows behind the high altar relate biblical stories about the prophets and saints as well as the life and Passion of Jesus.

⑤ High Altar
Stephansdom's beautiful Baroque high altar **(above)** was created by the brothers Tobias and Johann Pock in 1647. The painting in the centre of the marble altar depicts the stoning of the cathedral's patron saint, St Stephen.

② Organ
There has been an organ in the cathedral since 1334. The west choir organ **(above)**, with 125 stops and 10,000 pipes, was installed in the loft above the entrance in 1960.

⑥ Vaulting
The magnificent Gothic main nave of the cathedral is covered by an impressive ribbed vault supported by tall pillars.

7 North Tower with Pummerin

The North Tower, topped with a cupola, is home to the huge Pummerin bell. Weighing 21 tonnes, this great bell was cast from 100 cannons that were seized during the failed siege of Vienna by the Turks in 1683.

9 Catacombs

When Charles VI closed the cathedral cemetery in 1732, catacombs were built to bury the city's dead. By the end of the 18th century, about 11,000 people were laid to rest here. The Duke's Crypt has urns containing the organs of the Habsburg family.

10 West Front

The two imposing Romanesque Heathen Towers that flank the Giant's Door (above), and the two Gothic side chapels, with their filigree stone rose windows, are a spectacular welcome to the cathedral.

Stephansdom

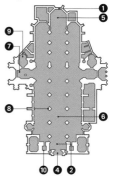

8 Pillars

The main nave of Stephansdom is dominated by soaring pillars, lavishly decorated with 77 clay and stone statues dating back to the 15th century.

NEED TO KNOW

MAP N3 ■ Stephansplatz ■ 01 515 52 3054 ■ www. stephanskirche.at

Open 6am–10pm Mon–Sat, 7am–10pm Sun

Tours (English): 10:30am Mon–Sat

South Tower: stairs open 9am–5:30pm daily; adm €5

North Tower: lift open 9am–5:30pm daily; adm €6

Catacombs: open 10–11:30am & 1–4:30pm Mon–Sat, 1–4:30pm Sun & public hols; adm €6

■ Access to the Catacombs is by guided tour only.

■ You can climb 343 steps to the top of the South Tower, or take a lift up the North Tower, for stunning views over the rooftops.

Cathedral Guide
Enter through the Giant's Door. The Gothic pulpit and North Tower lift are to your left. The catacombs' entrance is in the middle of the left side. In the far right corner is the raised tomb of Friedrich III (see p14).

Gothic Features in the Cathedral

1 Master Pilgram
A self-portrait of Master Anton Pilgram – one of the key craftsmen that worked on the cathedral – can be seen at the base of the old organ. He is holding his tools – a pair of compasses in his right hand and a set square in his left hand.

2 Fenstergucker
In this marvellous example of the Viennese late Gothic period, a sculpture of Master Pilgram himself leans out of an open window below the pulpit steps to inspect his work.

Gothic Features in the Cathedral

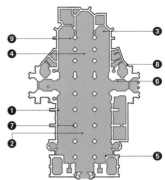

Fenstergucker below the pulpit

3 Raised Tomb of Friedrich III
Friedrich III commissioned Niklas Gerhaert van Leyden to create a majestic raised tomb for him. It took 45 years to build and was finished 20 years after the emperor's death. Little carved monks along the sarcophagus pray for his soul.

4 Baptismal Basin
Carved from red Salzburg marble, it took five years to finish this incredibly ornate 14-sided basin. Its decorations depict the seven holy sacraments, in the centre of which is Jesus's baptism.

5 Canopy with Pötscher Madonna
The 16th-century stone canopy shelters an icon of the Madonna from the Hungarian village of Máriapócs. In the 17th century the story spread that tears ran down Mary's cheeks and today people pray here for the sick to be healed.

6 Servants' Madonna
The graceful statue of the Madonna and Child is said to have miraculously helped acquit a maid who had been wrongly accused of stealing valuables from her master.

7 Pulpit
The lavishly decorated pulpit was created by Anton Pilgram in 1510. Lizards and toads, symbolizing evil, crawl up the balustrade, but they are fought off by a dog, the symbol of good.

Stephansdom's elaborate pulpit

JOHANNES CAPISTRANUS AND THE TURKISH SIEGE

On the northeastern exterior wall of the cathedral is an elaborate Baroque pulpit cast in honour of Franciscan saint Johannes Capistranus (1385–1456). Born in Italy, Johannes left a legal career after having a dream in which St Francis urged him to join the Franciscan Order. He became a priest in 1425 and soon huge crowds flocked to hear him preach against heresy all over Italy. But it was for his peacemaking skills that he was best known. After missions in Italy and France, he was sent to Austria in 1451 to preach against the Turkish invasion, and he led the Christian army to victory against the Turks in the battle of Belgrade in 1456. Johannes was canonized in 1724; the Austrians erected the pulpit in thanks later that century.

Johannes Capistranus' pulpit

TOP 10 EVENTS IN THE CATHEDRAL'S HISTORY

1 The first church on the site is consecrated (1147)

2 St Stephen's gains the status of a diocese (1469)

3 Double wedding of Maximilian's grand-children to the children of the Hungarian king (1515)

4 Wolfgang Amadeus Mozart weds Constanze Weber (1782)

5 The catacombs are closed, due to a plague epidemic (1783)

6 Mozart's sudden death and modest funeral (1791)

7 "October Revolution" rages in and around Stephansdom (1848)

8 Emperor Franz Joseph's funeral (1916)

9 Fire destroys the cathedral's roof (1945)

10 Funeral of Zita, wife of the last Austrian emperor, Charles I (1989)

The 1916 funeral procession of Emperor Franz Joseph I was filmed en route to the cathedral.

⑧ Cenotaph of Rudolph the Founder

Rudolph the Founder and his wife Katharina lie next to each other on their marble sarcophagus. The tomb was originally decorated with gold and precious jewels, and figures were placed in the little alcoves.

⑨ Wiener Neustädter Altar

The richly decorated altar just to the left of the main altar has four wings and shows 72 saints and scenes from the life of the Virgin Mary. Carved and painted in 1447, it was originally used as a shrine for relics.

Gargoyles at the top of the cathedral

⑩ Gargoyles

The gargoyles on the exterior roof of the cathedral are made in the shape of dragons and other mythical animals in order to ward off evil.

TOP 10 ⭐ The Hofburg

The Hofburg, Vienna's former imperial palace, is a lavish complex of buildings spread over a large area within the city centre. Once home to emperors, the medieval castle was further enlarged gradually up until 1918, and as the power of the Habsburgs grew, successive emperors added buildings – the Neue Burg (New Palace) is its most recent and grand section. Today the Hofburg houses the offices of the Austrian president, a convention centre, museums, state rooms and the Winter Riding School where the elegant white Lipizzaner stallions of the Spanish Riding School perform.

1 Swiss Gate
The name of this Renaissance gate **(above)** refers to the Swiss guards that were employed by Empress Maria Theresa in the 18th century.

NEED TO KNOW

MAP L4 ■ Innerer Burghof/ Kaisertor ■ Adm €16 ■ www. sisimuseum-hofburg.at

Imperial Apartments: open Sep–Jun: 9am–5:30pm daily; Jul & Aug: 9am–6pm daily

Spanish Riding School: 01 533 90 31; guided tours daily; morning exercises 10am–noon

■ Every Sunday, the Vienna Boys' Choir performs at 9:15am in the Imperial Chapel. Book tickets in advance.

2 Austrian National Library
The Baroque library was built between 1723 and 1726 by Josef Emanuel Fischer von Erlach. It has a priceless collection of historic manuscripts in walnut bookcases.

3 Imperial Silver Collection
The elaborate serving bowl, table decorations and silverware in this collection show the splendour that marked meals at the imperial court.

The Hofburg

6 Heroes' Square

Prince Eugene of Savoy and Archduke Charles' equestrian statues **(left)** dominate Heldenplatz (Heroes' Square), formerly a parade ground.

7 Secular and Ecclesiastical Treasuries

Magnificent artifacts are on display in 16 rooms dedicated to the relics of the Austrian and Holy Roman empires.

BUILDING THE PALACE

Every emperor left his mark on the palace until 1918. The Stallburg was built in the Renaissance under Maximilian II, while Amalienburg, constructed for his son Rudolph II, was completed in 1605. The oldest surviving part is the Schweizertrakt, featuring the Imperial Chapel and the Swiss Gate (1552–3).

8 Burggarten and Volksgarten

Both of these pretty parks **(above)** owe their origins to the Napoleonic troops who blew up parts of the palace in 1809, creating open spaces.

9 Imperial Chapel

Although the original interior with carved statuary was altered by Maria Theresa, the Burgkapelle (Royal Chapel) remains one of the oldest parts of the palace. Musicians including Mozart gave recitals here.

10 Imperial Apartments

The Kaiserappartements (private apartments) in the Amalia Wing are preserved as they were in the day of Franz Joseph and his wife Elisabeth *(see p19)*. Six rooms are dedicated to her as the Sisi Museum **(below)**.

4 Michaeler Gate

The majestic Michaeler Gate **(above)** is the main entrance into the complex, and its imposing green dome with golden decorations looms over Michaelerplatz.

5 Museums

The semicircular Neue Burg, with its vast colonnaded façade, is home to collections of musical instruments, arms and armour, and the Weltmuseum Wien ethnological museum.

Artistic Treasures in the Hofburg

1 Crown of the Holy Roman Empire

Featured in the palace's collection of ecclesiastical and secular precious objects is this gold crown, decorated with gemstones and cloisonné enamel. It was crafted in around AD 962.

Bejewelled gold crown

2 Musical Instruments

The impressive Sammlung Alter Musikinstrumente houses a collection of Renaissance and Baroque musical instruments, as well as pianos that belonged to Beethoven, Schubert and Haydn.

3 Austrian Sceptre and Orb

The enthroning of a new Habsburg ruler was accompanied by a cere-mony of homage, during which the sovereign carried the sceptre and orb.

4 The Golden Fleece

This chainmail armour, made in 1517, consists of a neck chain and a collar of double-walled plates.

5 Austrian National Library Frescoes

Artist Daniel Gran painted these frescoes in the main hall in 1730 in honour of Emperor Charles VI. The statue here depicts the emperor as the centre of the universe, holding a balance between war and peace.

6 Captain Cook Artifacts

Among the exhibits in the Weltmuseum Wien ethnological museum are artifacts acquired by British explorer Captain James Cook on his voyages around the globe, including masks from North America.

Ornate cradle of the King of Rome

7 Cradle of the King of Rome

This cradle was given by Maria Louisa, Archduchess of Austria and second wife of Napoleon, to her son, the King of Rome. It is adorned with gold, silver and mother-of-pearl, while a goddess of victory crowns the child with a diadem of stars and a laurel wreath.

8 Aztec Feather Headpiece

The Penacho is the only one of its kind in exis-tence today. Restoration of the 450 green-tail Quetzal feathers and 1,000 gold plates was a joint project with Mexico.

National Library

9 Portrait of Empress Elisabeth

German painter and renowned court portraitist Franz Xavier Winterhalter painted this famous portrait of the Empress Elisabeth in 1865. It hangs in one of the rooms of the Sisi Museum *(see p17)*.

10 Silverware and Porcelain

The *Silberkammer* displays the silverware and Vienna porcelain that was used for imperial banquets. This exhibit offers visitors a unique insight into courtly dining customs.

Impressive silverware collection

FRANZ JOSEPH AND SISI

Born in 1830, Franz Joseph was crowned Emperor of Austria in 1848, aged 18. He met his wife, Princess Elisabeth of Bavaria, lovingly known to Austrians as "Sisi", in 1853 and they married shortly after. The empress was adored by Austrians, then as now, for her extraordinary beauty, dignity and elegance in state matters. Many believed Franz Joseph's social successes were the result of Sisi's influence, and they considered her their "real" sovereign. The lives of the emperor and empress were not without trials and sorrows, however. Franz Joseph lost major wars to France (1848) and Prussia (1866), despite being crowned King of Hungary in 1867. They also suffered many personal

Empress Elisabeth

tragedies – the emperor's brother, Maximilian, was executed in Mexico and his only son, Crown Prince Rudolph, committed suicide in 1889, after which Sisi dressed only in black. Austria, too, fell into mourning in 1898 when their beloved empress was assassinated in Geneva. Franz Joseph ruled for 68 years, until his death in 1916.

TOP 10 EVENTS IN THE HOFBURG

1 A fort is built on the site of today's Hofburg (1275)

2 The Alte Burg wing is built under Ferdinand I (1547–52)

3 Fischer von Erlach starts building the Winter Riding School (1729)

4 Carousels with the Lipizzaner horses are staged in the Winter Riding School (1740–80)

5 Mozart gives musical performances regularly in the Burgkapelle between 1781 and 1791

6 The Vienna Congress is held (1815)

7 The Michaeler wing is built (1889–93)

8 World War I prevents the completion of the Neue Burg (1918)

9 Hitler proclaims the annexation of Austria to the Third Reich from the balcony of Neue Burg (1938)

10 Fire destroys the ballroom in the Redoute wing (1992)

Spanish Riding School

Spanish Riding School horses and riders at the Winter Riding School

1 Horses' Steps

The steps of the famous white Lipizzaner stallions of the Spanish Riding School follow the rigid patterns of the "high art" of riding which was established during the Renaissance period. Agility and strength are the goals. The most difficult part of the performance is the quadrille, which involves a precise and exact framework of choreography.

2 Emperor's Box

Once reserved for the imperial family, the royal box still has the best seats in the house.

Riders in the Emperor's box

3 Portrait of Charles VI

A portrait of Charles VI riding on a white stallion hangs in the royal box. Riders entering the hall pay respect to the founder of the school by raising their bicorn hats to the painting.

4 Lipizzaner Horses

The elegant white Lipizzaner stallions are bred at the national stud farm at Piber. The foals are born dark-skinned or black and acquire their trademark white coat between the ages of four and ten.

Lipizzaner horse and rider

5 Training

The horses move from the stud farm to the Spanish Riding School when they are about four years old and are then trained for a minimum of eight years, or until they are skilled enough to perform.

6 Riders

Just like the horses, the riders at the school have to go through an extensive training period before they can perform classical dressage and other riding techniques. The riders traditionally wear white jodhpurs and a double-breasted coffee-brown coat with brass buttons.

7 Stables
This Renaissance building in the Stallburg section of the Hofburg has an impressive three-storey gallery. It was built during the reign of Emperor Maximilian II.

8 Winter Riding School
Since 1735 the Spanish Riding School has been located in the Winter Riding School building, designed by Fischer von Erlach in Baroque style.

9 Interior
The horses perform their elegant ballet in the 56-m- (180-ft-) long hall. The gallery here is supported by 46 Corinthian columns.

10 Summer Riding School
During the summertime, performances and training sessions at the Spanish Riding School are carried out in a courtyard adjoining the Winter Riding School.

THE HISTORY OF THE LIPIZZANER HORSES

Spanish horses were first brought to Austria from Spain by Emperor Maximilian II in 1562, and the first evidence of them being housed in the Spanish Riding School dates back to 1572. In 1580, the horses were given the name Lipizzaner after a stud farm in Trieste; around this time the first riding hall was built at the present location. The school we know today was formed in the 19th century and hosted equestrian events where the horses performed in graceful formations. For 436 years, riders were exclusively male. In 2008, two women, one Austrian and one British, were accepted into the school. Riding costumes have remained unchanged from the "Empire Style" of 1795.

TOP 10 PIECES OF TACK AND DRESS

1 Bicorn Napoleon hats
2 Brown cut-away tailcoats
3 Buckskin breeches
4 Knee-high black boots
5 Swan neck spurs
6 Buckskin saddle
7 Pale suede gloves
8 Gold-plated bridles
9 Saddlecloth colour indicates status of rider
10 Gold-plated horse breastplate

This late 19th-century painting, *Morning Training in the Winter Riding School* (1890) by Italian painter Julius von Blaas, shows several of the graceful stallions practising their exercises in the elegant surroundings of the riding school.

🔟 ⭐ Kunsthistorisches Museum

Built in Italian Renaissance style by architects Karl von Hasenauer and Gottfried Semper, the impressive Kunsthistorisches Museum was opened in 1891. The majestic architecture creates a fitting setting for the artistic treasures assembled by the Habsburgs, who were enthusiastic patrons and collectors for centuries. The museum's collections, particularly the Old Masters, are among the most important and spectacular found anywhere in the world.

1 Large Self-Portrait

The Dutch master artist Rembrandt painted this canvas in 1652, depicting everything around him in dark colours, with his face the only area of light.

3 Blue Hippo

Hippo figurines are often found in the tombs of Ancient Egypt, as they were thought to help gain entry into the afterlife. This one *(see p24)* has drawings of plants from the Nile Delta on its body.

4 Virgin and Child with a Pear

German artist Albrecht Dürer (1471–1528) painted many Madonna pictures, but this one **(left)** is among the best known. It shows the Virgin Mary bending over a child holding a pear core.

2 Peasant Wedding

More than any of his other works, this 1568 painting **(below)** contributed to Pieter Brueghel the Elder's fame as a portrayer of peasant life. The viewer feels right in the middle of a rustic wedding.

5 The Fur

This 1638 painting **(above)** is the most intimate portrait of Peter Paul Rubens' wife Hélène, whom he married late in life and whose features he often incorporated into his works. In a naturally graceful pose, the young woman evokes Venus, goddess of love.

6 Maria Theresa's Breakfast Service

Crafted in Vienna around 1750, this pure gold set belonged to the empress and consists of about 70 pieces, including a stunning gold teapot. Some items, such as a mirror and a basin, are part of a washing set.

7 St Gregory with the Scribes

A late-9th-century ivory carving from Germany **(left)** showing St Gregory and three scribes.

8 Madonna of the Cherries

A number of paintings by Titian can be found in the Italian Collection. In this one (1518), the Madonna's dress is painted in the red-brown colours for which the artist is known.

9 Summer

From 1562, Italian Giuseppe Arcimboldo served as portrait artist at the court of Rudolph II. He became famous for his heads composed of fruits and vegetables **(below)** which served as allegorical representations.

10 Stela of Ha-hat, Thebes

The stela (stone slab), which is more than 2,500 years old, is lavishly painted in gold, red and blue and depicts Osiris among other Egyptian gods, who are praised in the inscriptions. The stela was discovered inside a tomb in Thebes.

Kunsthistorisches Museum

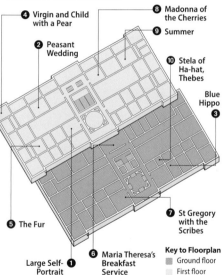

- **4** Virgin and Child with a Pear
- **2** Peasant Wedding
- **8** Madonna of the Cherries
- **9** Summer
- **10** Stela of Ha-hat, Thebes
- **3** Blue Hippo
- **5** The Fur
- **7** St Gregory with the Scribes
- **1** Large Self-Portrait
- **6** Maria Theresa's Breakfast Service

Key to Floorplan
■ Ground floor
■ First floor

NEED TO KNOW

MAP K5 ■ Maria-Theresien-Platz ■ 01 525 240 ■ www.khm.at

Open 10am–6pm Tue–Sun (until 9pm Thu)

Adm €18 (under 19s free)

■ Audio guides priced at €6 (€8 for two) are available at the museum.

■ Don't forget to admire the stunning view of the white marble floor with black patterns from the café on the first floor.

Museum Guide

The main entrance is on Maria-Theresien-Platz. As you enter, collect a map to guide you. On the ground floor are the Egyptian Collection and the Greek and Roman Antiquities to your right, while the left wing hosts the magnificent Kunstkammer (Chamber of Art and Wonders). The stairs lead to the Picture Gallery where some of the most famous paintings are located. The Coin Cabinet and Vermeyen cartoons are on the second floor.

The Kunsthistorisches Collections

1 The Vermeyen Cartoons

These large cartoons, or sketches, depict various scenes from Emperor Charles V's Tunis campaign of 1535. They were produced by court painter Jan Cornelisz Vermeyen (who accompanied the emperor on the campaign). Willem de Pannemaker used them as models for 12 tapestries that now hang in Madrid.

The Kunsthistorisches Collections

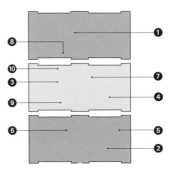

Key to Floorplan
- Ground floor
- First floor
- Second floor

Detail from a Vermeyen cartoon

2 Egyptian Collection

This section has a remarkably extensive stock of pieces from the Old and Middle Kingdoms of Ancient Egypt. The collection was amassed in the 19th and 20th centuries, developed by purchases, donations and new acquisitions from excavations.

3 Flemish Collection

A great number of works from 17th-century Flanders made their way into the museum because of Habsburg family ties to this part of Europe. The highlights are works by Rubens and Jan van Eyck.

4 Spanish and French Collection

Thanks to Habsburg family ties, portraits of the Spanish royal family form part of the collection. Diego Velázquez's portraits of the Infanta Margarita Teresa (daughter of Philip IV) are on display.

5 Greek and Roman Antiquities

The collection, originating from the former estate of the Habsburgs, covers a period of history extending from 3rd-century-BC Cypriot Bronze Age pottery to Slavic finds from the beginning of the 1st century AD. It is also internationally renowned as the home of the unique cameos and archaeological treasures dating from the Great Migration and the Early Middle Ages.

Ancient Egyptian blue hippo

6 Kunstkammer (Chamber of Art and Wonders)

Completely redesigned in 2013, this magnificent collection was amassed by emperors and archdukes in the Renaissance and Baroque periods. The Kunstkammer has 20 galleries and 2,200 pieces, and is justifiably known as "a museum within a museum". Natural objects to which were ascribed magical powers vie with masterpieces such as Maria Theresa's breakfast service *(see p22)* and the celebrated *Saliera* (salt cellar) by Benvenuto Cellini.

7 Italian Collection

The majority of the 15th- to 18th-century Italian paintings were collected by Archduke Leopold Wilhelm, who founded the collection in the 17th century. They are mainly from the Venetian Renaissance period, with major works by Titian, Veronese, Canaletto and Tintoretto.

Holbein's portrait of Jane Seymour

9 German Collection

The German collection has many 16th-century paintings. Among them are works by Dürer, Cranach the Elder and Holbein the Younger.

8 Coin Cabinet

There are more than 700,000 coins, medals and banknotes from three millennia on display in this fascinating numismatic collection.

Coin Cabinet exhibit

10 Dutch Collection

This section (15th to 17th century) includes a large collection of works by Pieter Brueghel the Elder, containing about a third of all his surviving pictures.

Crucifixion Triptych (c 1445) by Rogier van der Weyden in the Dutch Collection

Following pages Naiad Fountain at Schloss Schönbrunn

🔟⭐ The Belvedere

Prince Eugene of Savoy won his spurs at the relief of Vienna in 1683 and later regained large territories from the Turks. He commissioned the two Belvedere palaces with money he had received as a reward for his victories during the War of the Spanish Succession. The payment allowed him to carry out one of the most ambitious building projects ever undertaken by a private individual. The palaces were built by Lukas von Hildebrandt in 1714–23 as the prince's summer residence and are a shining example of Baroque style.

1 Upper Belvedere

Built to impress, and never inhabited, this elaborate palace (above) houses the greatest collection of Austrian art in the world, dating from medieval times to today.

2 Marble Hall

The most beautiful room within the Upper Belvedere, this has a lavish frescoed ceiling (below). The Austrian State Treaty was signed here in 1955.

3 Sala Terrena

Set on the ground floor, beneath the Marble Hall, is the beautiful Sala Terrena hall, with four massive statues supporting the vaulted ceiling. White stuccowork covers the walls and ceiling.

4 Lower Belvedere

The opulent Baroque palace, set in beautiful landscaped gardens, was the former living quarters and state rooms of Prince Eugene. It now houses special exhibitions only.

5 Marble Gallery

Constructed with niches to hold classical statues, this grandiose room has a stucco ceiling showing a heroic Prince Eugene being honoured.

6 Orangery and Palace Stables

Adjacent to the Lower Belvedere, the Orangery is a modern white exhibition space. The Stables feature examples of different painting styles.

8 Gold Cabinet

A statue of Prince Eugene of Savoy stands in this Lower Belvedere room (above). The walls are entirely covered by huge gilt-framed mirrors.

9 Belvedere 21

This Modernist building (see p123) was Austria's pavilion for Expo 58 (Brussels' World Fair in 1958). It was moved to Vienna and is now a museum of contemporary art. It also has an interesting cinema and workshop programme.

7 French Gardens

The Baroque gardens and terraces include the private flowers of Prince Eugene and Europe's oldest alpine gardens.

10 Garden Statues

Of the numerous statues dotted around the gardens, the Eight Muses and the Sphinxes (right) are the most outstanding.

The Belvedere

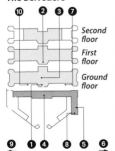

Second floor
First floor
Ground floor

Key to Floorplan
Upper Belvedere
Lower Belvedere

Artworks in the Belvedere

1 Napoleon at the Saint Bernard Pass

Jacques-Louis David's idealized rendering of Napoleon (1803) depicts him crossing the Alps into Italy in 1801 on a white stallion. In fact, Bonaparte made this journey on a mule.

2 Still Life with Dead Lamb

Seen as a metaphor of a world that has lost its way, this still life (1910) is one of the most important works by Oskar Kokoschka.

3 Adolescentia

Russian-born Elena Luksch-Makowsky was the first female member of the Vienna Secession and this painting is one of her finest. Depicting the transition from childhood to adulthood, *Adolescentia* (1903) is a striking example of the Secessionist style. She also designed enamel jewellery and mosaics for the Wiener Werkstätte (a design workshop linked to the Vienna Secession).

4 Character Heads

Franz Xavier Messerschmidt was one of the most eccentric artists of the 18th century. His "Character Heads" (1770–83) series presents busts with extreme facial expressions. Among the highlights is the amusing *Intentional Jester.*

Artworks in the Belvedere

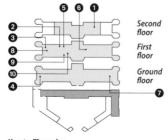

Key to Floorplan
- ▢ Upper Belvedere
- ▮ Lower Belvedere

Gerstl's *Self-Portrait, Laughing*

5 Self-Portrait, Laughing

Painted the same year that he committed suicide (1908), Richard Gerstl tries a last attempt at defiant self-definition.

6 The Chef

Claude Monet painted only a few portraits. This 1882 work (also known as *Le Père Paul*) shows the renowned chef Paul Antoine Graff, who owned a small hotel on the Normandy coast at which Monet stayed. Monet's depiction of the 60-year-old wearing a chef's hat and whites captures his facial expression with skilful spontaneity.

7 Znaimer Altarpiece

The carved inner sides of this magnificent triptych (c 1427) depict the events of Good Friday as recorded in the Gospel of St Matthew. The story is supplemented by scenes taken from the Apocrypha.

8 The Kiss

Painted in 1909, Gustav Klimt's most celebrated work, *The Kiss,* features the linear style and organic forms that would characterize the work of the Secessionists.

9 Death and the Maiden

A man and a woman are clutching each other on a sheet spread over uneven terrain in this painting (1915). Artist Egon Schiele painted his own features on the man.

10 Farmhouse in Upper Austria

Although Klimt is largely known for his figure paintings, landscapes also played a key part in his work. From 1900 he spent most summers in the Salzkammergut, painting scenes such as this (1911).

Klimt's *Farmhouse in Upper Austria*

THE SECESSIONIST MOVEMENT

Formed in 1897, the Secessionist style was a reaction against the conservative "historicism" of the Association of Austrian Artists, Vienna's dominant artistic union, which still flourishes and today occupies the Albertina Modern *(see p59)*. The leader and first president of the breakaway Union of Austrian Artists was Gustav Klimt. Members included Koloman Moser, Josef Hoffmann, Max Kurzweil, Elena Luksch-Makowsky and Wilhelm Bernatzik. Architect Otto Wagner joined later. The group was called the "Vienna Secession", as their movement followed similar rebellions in Berlin and Munich. Secessionism has no single defining stylistic theme, aside from the desire to eliminate historical influences. Their masterpiece is the Secession Building *(see pp38–9)*.

TOP 10 AUSTRIAN 19TH- AND 20TH-CENTURY ARTISTS

1 Gustav Klimt (1862–1918)

2 Kolo Moser (1868–1918)

3 Richard Gerstl (1883–1908)

4 Oskar Kokoschka (1886–1980)

5 Egon Schiele (1890–1918)

6 Maria Lassnig (1919–2014)

7 Friedensreich Hundertwasser (1928–2000)

8 Kiki Koglenik (b 1935)

9 Christian Ludwig Attersee (b 1940)

10 Martha Neuwirth (b 1940)

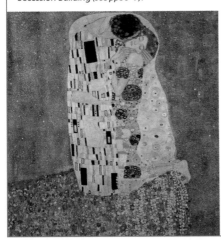

Klimt's glittering, erotic work, *The Kiss* was inspired by the golden mosaics he saw while visiting Ravenna and Venice in Italy. He adapted the idea into what is now his most widely recognized painting.

🔟 ⭐ Karlskirche

St Charles' Church was built between 1715 and 1737 to honour Karl Borromeo, patron saint of the fight against the plague. The aim was to thank God for delivering Vienna from the epidemic in 1713 that had claimed more than 8,000 lives. Emperor Charles held a competition among architects to design the church, which was won by Johann Fischer von Erlach. The architectural masterpiece has a dome and portico borrowed from classical Greek architecture, while the two tower pavilions show the influence of Roman Baroque.

4 Cupola with Frescoes

The fresco by Johann Michael Rottmayr on the interior of the dome depicts the Virgin Mary begging the Holy Trinity to deliver the population from the plague.

5 Pediment Reliefs

The pediment resembles the covering of a Greek temple. Its artful reliefs, designed by Giovanni Stanetti, show the suffering of the Viennese during the 1713 plague.

1 Altar Paintings

The side altars feature several paintings, but the most remarkable are those by master artist Daniel Gran **(above)**. His famous paintings *The Healing of a Gout Victim*, *Jesus and the Roman Captain* and *Saint Elisabeth of Hungary* can be found in the church.

2 Karl Borromeo Statue

Designed by Lorenzo Mattielli, this statue of the patron saint of the fight against the plague sits on the church's pediment.

3 Entrance

The stunning façade **(below)** is winged by two gatehouses that are built in a style similar to that of Chinese pavilions and lead into the side entrances. At the centre of the façade is the stairway, atop which is a Classical pediment supported by six pillars.

6 Columns

Inspired by the ancient Roman column of Trajan, the church's two huge columns are decorated with scenes from the life of St Karl Borromeo. The left column shows the quality of steadfastness, while the column on the right shows courage.

NEED TO KNOW

MAP F4 ▪ 01 505 62 94 ▪ Karlsplatz ▪ www.karlskirche.at

Open 9am–6pm Mon–Sat, noon–7pm Sun & holidays

Adm €8 (including lift)

▪ Take the lift to the top of the dome to get a look at the frescoes on its interior and to enjoy the amazing city views.

JOHANN FISCHER VON ERLACH

Many of Vienna's finest buildings were designed by Johann Fischer von Erlach (1656–1723). The Graz-born architect studied in Rome, and then moved to Vienna, where he became the court architect and a leading exponent of the Baroque style. He designed a great many churches and palaces, notably Karlskirche and the university church at Salzburg. Moreover, he sketched the initial plans for Schönbrunn Palace *(see pp42–5)*. After Erlach's death in Vienna, Karlskirche was completed by his son.

9 Pulpit
Atop the church's richly gilded pulpit are two cherubs on the canopy and it is decorated with *rocailles* (scrolls) and garlands of flowers.

7 High Altar
The high altar **(above)**, designed in typical Baroque style, was probably planned by Fischer von Erlach himself. It features a stucco relief by Albert Camesina illustrating St Karl Borromeo being carried into heaven on a cloud laden with angels and cherubs.

8 Pond with Henry Moore Sculpture
The church's setting is as impressive as its interior. In front of the church lies a stone-paved pond atop which rests a bronze Henry Moore sculpture. The modern figure contrasts sharply with the ornate Baroque style of the church.

10 Angels
Two angels guard the exterior stairway. The angel on the right represents the New Testament; the one on the left **(below)**, the Old Testament.

Karlskirche

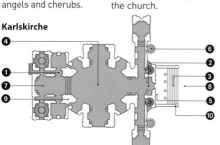

📺🔟 ⭐ MuseumsQuartier

Today one of Europe's most vibrant cultural complexes, the Museum Quarter's first buildings, some 300 years ago, were stables, home to the emperor's horses. They were commissioned by Charles VI in 1713 and completed by Johann Fischer von Erlach in 1725, with the stables being transformed into an exhibition ground in 1918. The MQ, as it is called, now houses more than 70 cultural centres, in varying styles, with shops and restaurants. In summer, the main courtyard is filled all day and night. Underground parking, free Wi-Fi and a maze of passageways opening into seven art-filled courtyards attract more than four million visitors a year.

1 mumok
The grey basalt lava building **(above)** is home to a collection of 20th-century masterpieces *(see p59)*.

2 ZOOM
An exciting place **(below)** for kids aged eight months to 14 years. Children are encouraged to learn with fun-filled painting and activities *(see p69)*.

3 Q21
Vienna's centre for contemporary applied art, Q21 stages numerous creative initiatives that are spread all over the MQ. Street art and daily exhibitions, as well as office and editing spaces for the artists in residence, are among its many programmes.

4 Kunsthalle
Considered the latest outpost of the contemporary art exhibition space on Karlsplatz *(see p59)*, Kunsthalle is host to frequently changing exhibitions featuring up and coming artists.

⑨ Tanzquartier Wien
Known as TQW, this dance centre is Austria's first dedicated performance and study venue focusing solely on modern dance.

⑥ Leopold Museum
The museum **(above)** has the world's biggest Egon Schiele collection, as well as paintings by Klimt.

⑦ Halle E+G
These two event halls host music, dance and musical theatre performances. The Baroque Halle E once housed horses.

⑧ wienXtra-kinderinfo
A play area for kids under 13 and information centre for parents, offering free advice on kids' activities in Vienna.

⑩ AzW
The Austrian Architecture Museum **(above)** has exhibits, regular lectures and an extensive academic library, as well as an impressive restaurant in the complex.

MuseumsQuartier

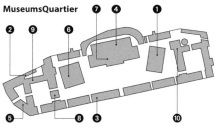

⑤ Dschungel
Vienna's theatre hub for kids and families features puppets, dance, film and even opera in two auditoriums.

NEED TO KNOW

MAP J5 ■ Museumsplatz 1 ■ 01 523 58 81 ■ www. mqw.at

mumok: open 2–7pm Mon, 10am–7pm Tue–Sun (until 9pm Thu); adm €15 (under 19s free); www.mumok.at

ZOOM: open 8:30am–4pm Tue–Fri, 9:45am–4pm Sat, Sun & public hols (Jul–Sep: 12:45–5pm daily); www. kindermuseum.at

Q21: open 10am–10pm daily; www.q21.at

Kunsthalle: open 11am–7pm Tue–Sun (until 9pm Thu); adm €8 (under 19s free); www.kunsthallewien.at

Dschungel: open 4–6pm Mon–Fri; www.dschungel wien.at

Leopold Museum: open 10am–6pm Wed–Mon (until 9pm Thu); adm €15; www.leopoldmuseum.org

Halle E+G: open 10am–1pm & 2–7pm Mon–Sat; www.halleneg.at

wienXtra-kinderinfo: open 2–6pm Tue–Fri, 10am–5pm Sat & Sun; www.wienxtra.at

Tanzquartier Wien: open 10am–6pm Mon–Fri; adm €20; www.tqw.at

AzW: open 10am–7pm daily; adm €9 (under 6s free); www.azw.at

TOP 10 ⭐ Staatsoper

As the first of the grand buildings on the Ringstrasse, construction of the Neo-Renaissance State Opera House began in 1861 under the architects Eduard van der Nüll and August von Siccardsburg, and opened in May 1869 with Mozart's *Don Giovanni*. However, the new opera house did not appeal to Emperor Franz Joseph, who referred to it as a "railway station", leading van der Nüll to commit suicide. In 1945 the Staatsoper was hit by World War II bombs and almost entirely destroyed. Following its restoration in 1955, the State Opera is the world's largest repertory theatre. Performances are held 300 nights of the year.

6 Grand Staircase

The magnificent marble staircase **(right)**, decorated with frescoes, mirrors and chandeliers, leads to the auditorium. Its arches are embellished with statues by Josef Gasser, depicting the seven liberal arts: architecture, poetry, dance, sculpture, art, music and drama.

1 Exterior

Seen from the Ringstrasse, the majestic pale stone building **(above)** is dominated by the original loggia, which survived World War II.

2 Bronze Statues

The large bronze statues, placed in the five arches of the loggia, are the creation of Ernst Julius Hähnel (1876) and are allegories of heroism, drama, fantasy, comedy and love, as seen from left to right.

3 Tea Salon

One of the most splendid rooms in the building is the Tea Salon. Its centrepiece is a fireplace flanked by pillars and mirrors.

4 Reliefs of Opera and Ballet

Created by Johann Preleuthner, two reliefs show the two genres performed in the house: opera and ballet.

5 Auditorium

Following its destruction in World War II, it was decided, after much discussion, that the auditorium **(below)** be rebuilt to its original 1869 design with three box circles and two open circles.

7 Tapestries

Nine tapestries in the Gustav Mahler Hall, designed by Rudolf Eisenmenger, show scenes from Mozart's opera *The Magic Flute*.

⑩ Schwind Foyer
In the superb Schwind Foyer are 16 oil paintings by Moritz von Schwind. They represent some famous operas, including Rossini's *The Barber of Seville* (1816) and Beethoven's *Fidelio* (1805). A bust of the composers is placed beneath each illustration.

NEED TO KNOW

MAP M5 ■ Opernring 2 ■ 01 514 44 2250 (tours); 01 514 447 880 (tickets) ■ www.wiener-staats oper.at

Open for pre-booked 40-minute guided tours only. Tour times vary and are usually scheduled around rehearsals.

Adm €13

■ All tickets for the upcoming season can be booked in advance.

■ Up to 25 tickets at €15 are reserved for children under 16.

■ Seats for selected performances cost €20 for those under 27.

■ Standing-room-only tickets are sold for €13 to €18, 80 minutes before curtain time.

⑧ Gustav Mahler Bust
The bronze bust of world-renowned composer Gustav Mahler, who served as director of the Vienna Court Opera from 1897 to 1907, was created by Auguste Rodin in 1909. It is placed in the Schwind Foyer, alongside busts of other "conducting directors" of the opera.

⑨ Fountains
The two imposing fountains **(left)** that can be seen on the right and left sides of the opera house were created by the famed Austrian sculptor Josef Gasser (1817–68). They represent two different worlds: music, dance, joy and levity on the left, and the siren Lorelei with love, revenge and sorrow, on the right.

TOP 10 ⭐ Secession Building

The large, white, cubic Secession Building was designed in 1897 by Joseph Maria Olbrich, the Austrian architect and co-founder of the Vienna Secession, as the manifesto of the late-19th-century art movement. The iconic exhibition hall opened in October 1898. The building was burned by retreating German forces during World War II and restoration began soon after in 1946. When first unveiled, the building was derided by the public, who called it "a greenhouse" and "a warehouse". Today it is one of the most treasured examples of a particularly Viennese artistic period.

1 Beethoven Frieze
Created by Gustav Klimt in 1902 for an exhibition paying homage to Ludwig van Beethoven, the 34-m- (110-ft-) long masterpiece **(above)** of Viennese Art Nouveau tells a story of the composer's Ninth Symphony, *Ode to Joy*.

2 Interior
The exhibition hall, in the shape of a basilica with a lofty nave and two lower aisles, can be easily adapted for each show staged here. Almost completely covered by a glass roof, by day it's bathed in a constant and even light.

3 Motto
Above the entrance of the pavilion is the gold motto of the Secessionist movement *"Der Zeit ihre Kunst. Der Kunst ihre Freiheit"* – "To every age its art, to art its freedom."

4 Flower Pots
The blue mosaic flowerpots **(right)** on either side of the entrance door are carried by four turtles. Their small trees add a touch of nature to smooth the building's hard lines.

5 Mark Anthony Statue
The bronze sculpture of the Roman general Mark Anthony in a chariot drawn by lions was created by Arthur Strasser in 1898. It was displayed at the fourth exhibition in the Secession and then set outside the building.

6 Dome
Made of 2,500 gilt laurel leaves and 311 berries, the dome is the most prominent feature of the design. The laurel symbolizes victory, dignity and purity.

7 Façade

Due to its huge, unbroken walls, the building **(above)** appears to be constructed from solid cubes.

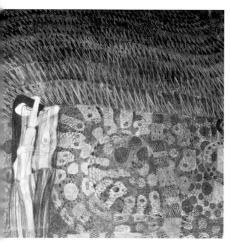

9 Architecture

The ground plan of the pavilion reveals simple geometrical forms, taking the square as the basic shape. The framework is softened by curves and ornaments.

10 Gorgons' Heads

The entrance is decorated with the heads of the three Gorgons **(below)**, which represent architecture, sculpture and painting. The sides also feature owls which, with the Gorgons, are virtues of Pallas Athena, Greek goddess of wisdom, victory and the crafts.

NEED TO KNOW

MAP L6 ■ Friedrichstrasse 12 ■ 01 587 53 07 ■ www.secession.at

Open 10am–6pm Tue–Sun

Guided tour (English) 11am Sat

Adm €9.50

■ For refreshments, try the trendy wine shop **Wien & Co Bar** *(see p118)* across the street from the Secession Building. A short stroll away from here will lead you to the **Café Museum** *(see p118)*, which serves coffee.

8 Ornaments

The building is decorated with gilt laurel garlands, floral patterns and plants along the sides of the walls. Most striking is the gold tree above the main door. These details contrast strikingly with the simplistic façade.

TOP 10 ⭐ Hundertwasserhaus

Opened in March 1986, this fairy-tale house with onion spires, green roof and a multicoloured façade is one of the city's most visited landmarks. Flamboyant Austrian artist Friedensreich Hundertwasser designed it as a playful take on usually dull social housing, in an attempt to show that practical could also be beautiful. Today almost 200 people live in the 50 apartments, each of which is individually decorated. Shrubs and trees on the balconies and roof gardens bring nature closer to city dwellers.

Façade ❶

The front of the house **(right)** is painted in bright shades of red, blue, yellow and white, and each of the differently coloured sections marks one apartment. The many trees growing in the rooftop gardens of the apartment block are also very unusual.

❷ Main Entrance

The building's main entrance, situated on Löwengasse, is an open section leading to the inner courtyard of the building. The apartments set just above the main entrance **(above)** are supported by colourful pillars. In front of the entrance is an attractive small fountain.

NEED TO KNOW

Kegelgasse 36–38
■ U-Bahn Landstrasse or trams 1 or O ■ www.hundertwasser-haus.info

■ The apartments at Hundertwasserhaus are private residences and can't be visited, but you can enjoy the building from one of the cafés in the complex, and stroll around the shops on the ground floor.

3 Onion Towers
Standing out amid the traditional city skyline, two golden glistening onion towers **(above)** sit atop the Hundertwasserhaus.

4 Irregular Windows
Hundertwasser believed that windows constitute a house's soul, so all the windows here vary in size and shape, and each of them is framed by a complementary colour.

5 Roof Gardens
Each apartment has access to a little piece of nature in the form of the roof gardens and balconies that are scattered all over the building. The gardens have some 250 large trees, trimmed shrubs and a grass lawn.

6 Ceramic Line
The size of every apartment is visible as it's marked by an uneven line of ceramic tiles **(below)**.

7 Decorations
The building is decorated with black, white and golden tiles. Statues on the corners of balconies, painted animals and plants on the corridor walls, and roof gardens give the place a cheerful appearance.

8 Pillars
A prominent feature of the structure is the range of brightly coloured, irregularly shaped shiny pillars **(above)**. Some of these pillars are integrated in the building and function as mere decoration, while others are more practical and are used to support the gallery that runs along the first floor of the block.

9 Glass Front
The two towers of the house – those crowned by the onion domes – host the central staircase. Thanks to the glass fronts, by day they are always light and airy.

10 Pavement
The area around Löwengasse is pedestrianized with some relaxed seating and elegant lampposts.

🔟⭐ Schloss Schönbrunn

The former summer residence of the Habsburgs, Schönbrunn Palace was built on land acquired by Maximilian II in 1569. At that time it was a wooded area outside the city. During the Turkish Siege of 1683, however, the woodland was destroyed, clearing the ground for this spectacular palace, built between 1695 and 1713 to the designs of the architect Johann Fischer von Erlach. Little of his original plans remain – Empress Maria Theresa ordered most of the interior to be redesigned in Late Baroque, or Rococo, style. The façade was altered in 1817–19, when it was painted in the characteristic "Schönbrunn yellow".

1 Grand Gallery

The 40-m- (130-ft-) long, 10-m- (30-ft-) wide gallery (above) has a stunning Rococo design of tall windows, splendid crystal mirrors, chandeliers and white-and-gold stucco. The Grand Gallery is still used for state receptions and banquets.

2 Porcelain Room

Maria Theresa's former study walls are covered with carved wooden frames painted blue and white to imitate porcelain.

3 Vieux-Laque Room

This room (left) unites Rococo elements with Chinese art: lacquer panels show landscapes adorned in gold. After her husband Francis I died in 1765, Maria Theresa hung portraits of him here as a memorial.

Schloss Schönbrunn

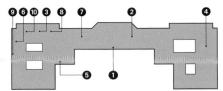

10 Napoleon's Room

When Napoleon occupied Vienna in 1805 and 1809 he stayed in this splendid room. Flemish tapestries from the 18th century adorn the walls.

4 Empress Elisabeth Salon

In Empress Elisabeth's Neo-Rococo reception room, there are portraits of Emperor Joseph I as a child and his sister Marie Antoinette.

5 Chapel

In 1740 Maria Theresa remodelled the chapel. The marble altar was designed by Georg Raphael Donner, and Paul Troger painted the ceiling fresco *The Marriage of the Virgin*.

6 Millions' Room

The name derives from the room's rose-wood panelling, which cost a reputed one million Gulden (former Austrian gold coins). In the panels, Indo-Persian miniatures illustrate scenes from the lives of the Mughal rulers of India in the 16th and 17th centuries.

8 Blue Chinese Salon

Decorated with Chinese paper wall hangings, this salon **(below)** was once the council chamber of Emperor Franz I Stephan.

9 Mirror Room

With magnificent white-and-gold Rococo decoration and crystal mirrors, this room is a fine example of Maria Theresa's style. Mozart once gave a private performance for the empress here.

7 Bergl Rooms

The garden rooms **(above)** were painted with frescoes by Johann Wenzl Bergl (1768–77) to satisfy Maria Theresa's taste for enchanting landscapes.

Features of Schönbrunn's Gardens

1 Schlosstheater
Commissioned by Maria Theresa, the theatre opened in 1747. The empress and her many children performed on the stage as singers.

2 Palmenhaus
The stunning steel-and-glass palm house was built in 1881–2 by Franz Xavier Segenschmid, using the latest technology. The central pavilion is 28 m (90 ft) high and has two wings.

Features of Schönbrunn's Gardens

Schönbrunn's Palmenhaus

3 Roman Ruins
Built in 1778, the Roman Ruins were designed to enhance the prestige and image of the Habsburgs by presenting them as the successors to the Roman emperors.

4 Gloriette
Situated at the summit of the park's hill, the magnificent Gloriette is its most prominent feature. The arcaded edifice was designed by architect Ferdinand Hetzendorf von Hohenberg in 1775 in Neo-Classical style and was once used as a dining hall before it became a viewing point, then later a café.

5 Beautiful Fountain
A fresh spring was discovered by Emperor Matthias while hunting in the area in 1619. In 1630, a well, together with a statue of a Roman nymph, was placed here, and it gave the palace its name (Schönbrunn is German for "beautiful fountain"). The fountain is close to the Roman Ruins.

6 Mythological Statues
The large park is dotted with 32 stone statues, created by Christian Beyer between 1753 and 1775. Each one represents a figure in Greek mythology or Roman history.

7 Wagenburg
A highlight of the Wagenburg (carriage museum) is the richly decorated imperial coach, which was built for the coronation of Joseph II in 1765. It was so heavy that eight horses were needed to pull it at walking pace.

The distinctive Gloriette arcade

EMPRESS MARIA THERESA AND SCHLOSS SCHÖNBRUNN

Most of the palace as it appears today was created during the reign of Empress Maria Theresa. She ascended the throne in 1740 after her father Charles VI changed the succession to enable females to rule Habsburg countries. The early years of her reign were characterized by foreign political failures as parts of Poland and Italy were lost in wars. But in domestic politics she introduced compulsory education, set up a new administrative structure and improved the social situation for farmers. Maria Theresa was impulsive in her younger years, but after the death of her husband Francis I in 1765 she wore only black mourning gowns and lived a sombre existence. She gave birth to 16 children, 10 of whom survived into adulthood.

TOP 10 RESIDENTS OF SCHLOSS SCHÖNBRUNN

1 Charles VI (1685–1740)

2 Maria Theresa (1717–80)

3 Francis I, husband of Maria Theresa (1708–65)

4 Marie Antoinette spent an idyllic childhood at Schönbrunn (1755–93)

5 Napoleon (1769–1821) used the palace as his headquarters in 1805 and 1809

6 Marie Louise, wife of Napoleon I (1791–1847)

7 Franz Josef Karl, Duke of Reichstadt, known as Napoleon II (1811–32)

8 Franz Joseph was born and died in the palace (1830–1916)

9 Elisabeth, wife of Franz Joseph (1837–98)

10 Rudolph (1858–89)

This portrait of Empress Maria Theresa by Josef Kiss and Friedrich Mayrhofer was painted in 1740, the year of her ascension to the throne.

8 Schönbrunn Park

The formal French Baroque park was laid out as a large pleasure garden by Nicolaus Jadot and Adrian von Steckhoven during the reign of Maria Theresa. It includes various architectural features.

9 Orangery

Schönbrunn's gardens are home to the second-largest Baroque orangery in the world. It was once used as winter quarters for orange trees and other potted plants, as well as for various imperial festivities.

10 Schönbrunn Zoo

Founded as early as 1752 as a royal menagerie by Emperor Franz I, this is the world's oldest zoo and is home to some 750 species.

Flamingos at Schönbrunn Zoo

The Top 10 of Everything

**Detail of the Art Nouveau altar
at Kirche am Steinhof**

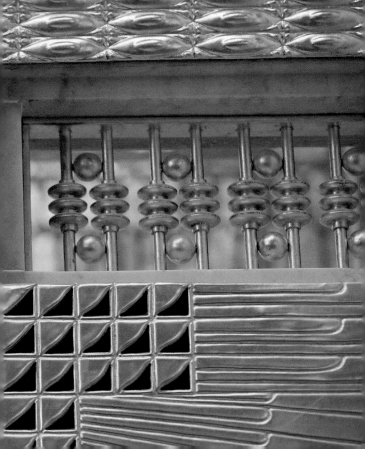

🔟 Moments in History

1 Founding
Early settlements in the area date back to the late Stone Age (5000 BC). The Celts later established the kingdom of Noricum in 200 BC. This was invaded by the Romans in 15 BC, who later set up a garrison, Vindobona, in AD 100. With the fall of the Roman Empire, control of the city changed hands. Finally, in AD 881, the name "Wenia" was first recorded.

2 Babenberg Rule
The Babenberg ruler Leopold was appointed Duke of the Eastern March in AD 976. By 1156, Vienna became the Babenbergs' main residence and developed into a centre of trade.

Stained-glass window of Rudolph I

3 Habsburg Rule
After the death of the last Babenberg and a spell of social disorder, the Habsburg Rudolph I was elected king in 1273. Vienna became the de facto centre of the Holy Roman Empire and a hub for arts, science and music. It remained the imperial city of the Habsburgs until 1918.

4 Turkish Siege
After Turkish troops failed to conquer Vienna in 1529, a huge army returned in 1683. The city was under siege for three months, but was liberated with the help of Polish troops. Prince Eugene finally destroyed the Ottoman Empire's influence with his victory in Belgrade in 1717.

5 Vienna Congress
After Napoleon was defeated in Leipzig (1813), the European powers met in Vienna in 1814–15 to make territorial decisions. The congress was attended by high-ranking delegates and glamorous balls were held.

6 1848 Revolution
A rigid political system under the state chancellor Metternich led to a period of calm and a rich, flourishing cultural life (1815–48). However, social discontent returned and ushered in a period of political upheaval in 1848. Upheavals reached a peak in October. Metternich was ousted from power and liberal ministers were appointed.

Painting of Vienna burning during the revolution in October 1848

7 End of the Austro-Hungarian Empire

With the death of Franz Joseph I in 1916, the Austro-Hungarian monarchy lost its uniting figure. Charles I, his successor, was not able to secure peace. The empire's defeat in World War I resulted in the Habsburgs losing both their lands and their crowns.

8 First Republic

When a new European map was drawn in 1918 at the end of World War I, the small Republic of Austria emerged. However, the country was struggling both economically and politically. Social unrest led to a civil war in February 1934, followed by a period of authoritarian rule.

German forces entering Vienna in 1938

9 Anschluss

Adolf Hitler marched on Vienna in March 1938 and declared Austria part of the Third Reich. Vienna was badly bombed during World War II, with many iconic landmarks destroyed.

10 Second Republic

In 1945, at the end of World War II, Vienna was divided into four zones occupied by the Allied powers (Great Britain, France, Russia and the US). In 1955, the last Allied soldiers left the country, and Austria regained full sovereignty with the signing of the State Treaty (see p29) in May.

TOP 10 HISTORICAL FIGURES

Empress Maria Theresa

1 Maria Theresa
The Empress (1717–80), known for her strong Catholic beliefs, modernized the empire by introducing many reforms.

2 Angelo Soliman
Formerly enslaved, Soliman (1721–96) later became highly respected in the city's intellectual circles.

3 Wolfgang Amadeus Mozart
One of the world's greatest composers, Mozart (1756–91) achieved fame in Vienna and created over 800 works.

4 Franz Joseph I
He came to power aged 18 and epitomized the monarchy as no other emperor before him (1830–1916).

5 Empress Elisabeth (Sisi)
Married at 16 to Franz Joseph I, the youthful Empress Elisabeth (1837–98) was assassinated in Geneva.

6 Otto Wagner
Many of Vienna's Art Nouveau buildings were designed by this acclaimed architect (1841–1918).

7 Bertha von Suttner
A pacifist and novelist, Bertha (1843–1914) was the first woman to win the Nobel Peace Prize.

8 Sigmund Freud
Freud (1856–1939), the founder of psychoanalysis, worked in Vienna before escaping to England.

9 Anna Sacher
Anna (1859–1930) took over the running of Hotel Sacher from her husband and made it one of Europe's most famous hotels.

10 Gustav Klimt
An icon of the Vienna Secession movement, Klimt (1862–1918) is most famous for his painting *The Kiss* (1908).

🔟 Places of Worship

The Neo-Classical interior of Griechisch-Orthodoxe Kirche

1 Griechisch-Orthodoxe Kirche

MAP N2 ▪ Fleischmarkt 13

In the early 18th century a Greek Orthodox community was founded in Vienna. After Emperor Joseph II issued a tolerance decree in 1787, the church on Fleischmarkt was built by Danish architect Theophil von Hansen. The pretty gold-and-red-striped building with arched windows was altered in Byzantine style in the mid-1900s.

2 Jesuitenkirche

MAP P3 ▪ Doktor-Ignaz-Seipel-Platz 1

Constructed at the beginning of the 17th century, the solemn façade of the Jesuitenkirche contrasts with its rich Baroque interior. Emperor Leopold I commissioned the Italian architect Andrea Pozzo to design the magnificent frescoes and paintings housed within the church. Pozzo also painted the barrel-vaulted ceiling so that the illusion of a dome was created.

3 Stephansdom

Sitting in the very heart of the city, this spectacular Gothic cathedral (see pp12–15) dominates the skyline.

4 Karlskirche

A stunning domed church (see pp32–3) that combines Classical and Baroque flourishes.

5 Votivkirche

The Votivkirche (see p102), an impressive sandstone church, was built between 1856 and

1879 in Neo-Gothic style to express gratitude that Franz Joseph survived an assassination attempt in 1853.

6 Michaelerkirche
MAP M3 ■ Michaelerplatz 4–5 ■ Guided tours of the crypt 11am & 1pm Mon–Sat ■ Adm

The imperial court attended masses in this church opposite the Hofburg palace. Originally Romanesque, it changed in style over the centuries after being rebuilt several times due to damage by fire. The original stone helmet of the tower, damaged after an earthquake, was replaced by a pointed roof in 1590. The portal is Baroque (1724–5) and the interior features Romanesque arcades and a Baroque high altar. The fascinating crypts *(see p62)* here are a huge draw.

7 Kirche am Steinhof
This fine Art Nouveau church *(see p127)* was designed by Otto Wagner and built in 1905–7 on the grounds of a psychiatric hospital. The square-shaped church with two bell towers and four angels over the door is overlooked by a golden dome that was converted to copper in the 1930s but has more recently been restored to its traditional hues. The window mosaics, designed by Kolo Moser, and a gilt altar canopy with angels delight those who enter the interior.

Art Nouveau Kirche am Steinhof

8 Wotruba-Kirche
Georgsgasse, corner of Rysergasse ■ Closed Mon–Fri

This unconventional church was built between 1974 and 1976 following designs by the Austrian sculptor Fritz Wotruba, who died shortly before the work was finished. It consists of 152 concrete cubes in various sizes that form a harmonious whole. In the spaces between the cubes, glass panes flood the interior with daylight.

Wotruba-Kirche's unusual building

9 Franziskanerkirche
MAP N4 ■ Franziskanerplatz

Located on the Franziskanerplatz *(see p94)*, the church and adjacent monastery of the Franciscan Order were constructed between 1603 and 1611 on the site of an older church. Dedicated to St Jerome, this is the city's only religious building with a Renaissance façade and a Baroque interior. It features six side altars in ornate recesses, a Baroque high altar (1707) by Andrea Pozzo, as well as Vienna's oldest organ (1642).

10 Maria am Gestade
MAP M2 ■ Salvatorgasse 12

This Gothic church, constructed on the site of a former wooden chapel, has an impressively slim west front, 33-m- (108-ft-) high and only 10-m- (30-ft-) wide. The tower is crowned by a white, open stone helmet (1394–1414) that once served as a landmark for Danube mariners. In a state of decay in the late 18th century, it was used as stables during the Napoleonic Wars but was restored in 1812.

🔟 Palaces and Historic Buildings

Baroque Gartenpalais Liechtenstein

1 Gartenpalais Liechtenstein

At the end of the 17th century the Liechtenstein family commissioned various architects to build them a summer residence. This impressive Baroque building *(see p101)* has been renovated and now houses the private art collection of the Liechtenstein family (mainly 17th-century art).

2 Palais Pallavicini
MAP M4 ■ Josefsplatz 5 ■ Closed to the public

Built at the site of the former Queen's Monastery between 1782 and 1784, this was Vienna's first Neo-Classical building, imitating ancient Greek as well as Roman architectural styles. The formal façade is enlivened by the striking portal with caryatids by Franz Anton von Zauner. The Pallavicini family still live here, and parts of the palace host a congress centre.

3 Augartenpalais
MAP B5 ■ Obere Augartenstrasse 1–3 ■ Closed to the public

The Baroque palace in Augarten park is now the home of the Vienna Boys' Choir school.

4 Palais Lobkowitz
MAP M4 ■ Lobkowitzplatz 2 ■ Open 10am–6pm Wed–Mon ■ Adm

Designed by Giovanni Pietro Tencalla, this large Baroque palace was built in 1685 as a stately city mansion for Count Dietrichstein. The Lobkowitz family acquired the palace in 1753. Today, the building is home to the Austrian Theatre Museum, which has exhibitions on costume design, ballet, opera and theatre. It also hosts stage readings and live performances.

5 Palais Schönborn-Batthyány
MAP L2 ■ Renngasse 4 ■ Closed to the public

The palace, designed by Fischer von Erlach between 1699 and 1706, was the home of the Hungarian Batthyány family, who fought for Prince Eugene *(see p48)*. The Schönborns acquired it in 1740; today it hosts classical music events.

6 Palais Ferstel
MAP L2 ■ Strauchgasse 4 ■ Closed to the public

This grand building in Historicist style was erected between 1856 and 1860 as a stock exchange for the National Bank. Now part of the palace is the Café Central *(see p98)*. The building is sometimes used for gala events.

Gilded arcade in Palais Ferstel

7 Dorotheum

The grand palace *(see p96)*, built in Neo-Baroque style between 1898 and 1901 by Emil Ritter von Förster, hosts pawnshops and one of Europe's largest auction houses.

8 Palais Daun-Kinsky
MAP L2 ■ Freyung 4 ■ Closed to the public

Baroque architect Johann Lukas von Hildebrandt's most splendid palace (1713–16) was acquired by the Kinsky family in 1784. Today, its lavish rooms host weddings and dinner events.

Lavish dining at Palais Daun-Kinsky

9 Palais Trautson
MAP J4 ■ Museumstrasse 7
■ Closed to the public

Count Trautson had this palace built in 1710–17 in French style; Maria Theresa converted it into guards' headquarters in 1760. Today it is used by the Austrian Justice Ministry.

10 Palais Mollard-Clary
MAP L2 ■ Herrengasse 9
■ Closed to the public

This 17th-century Baroque family mansion was used by Joseph II for his famous round table soirées. It now houses the Austrian Music Collection and the Globe Museum *(see p67)*.

TOP 10 EXAMPLES OF ARCHITECTURAL STYLES

1 Roman Houses
MAP L3 ■ Michaelerplatz
Early houses in parts of central Vienna were built by the Roman garrisons.

2 Medieval House
MAP P3 ■ Schönlaterngasse 7
The Basiliskenhaus is a fine example of a 13th-century home.

3 Renaissance
MAP N2 ■ Salvatorgasse 5
The portal of the Salvatorkapelle church dates back to 1530.

4 Baroque Palaces
Palaces built in richly decorated Baroque style can be found throughout Vienna, especially around the Ringstrasse.

5 Biedermeier House
MAP N5 ■ Annagasse 11
Arabesques and frescoes are typical of the Biedermeier period (1815–1848).

6 Art Nouveau Buildings
The stations of the former city railway *(see p122)* were constructed by Otto Wagner in the 1890s.

7 Purist Villa
Starkfriedgasse 19
The symmetrical Villa Moller by Adolf Loos (1927–8) reflects his principles of the use of space.

8 Council Housing
Heiligenstädter Strasse 82–92
The massive Karl-Marx-Hof building was constructed in 1930.

9 Haas-Haus
Designed by Hans Hollein in 1990, this Post-Modernist edifice is part-mirrored.

10 Gasometer
These gas storage towers were turned into apartments *(see p66)* in 2001.

Gasometer apartment block

🔟 Monuments and Memorials

1 Johann Strauss Monument

MAP P5 ■ Stadtpark, Parkring

Stadtpark *(see p64)* is dotted with monuments of artists and composers, but the gilded 1921 statue of Johann Strauss is allegedly the city's most photographed. The Viennese "Waltz King" is shown playing the violin amid ecstatic dancers and is framed by a marble arch.

Johann Strauss Monument, Stadtpark

2 Schubert's Grave

Zentralfriedhof, Simmeringer Hauptstrasse 234 ■ Tram 71

Franz Schubert was buried at the Währinger Friedhof on 21 November 1828, following his early death aged 31. When the cemetery was closed in 1872, his bones were moved to the Central Cemetery. There he was given an honorary grave among many of his composer friends.

3 Franz Schubert Monument

MAP Q4 ■ Stadtpark, Parkring

Franz Schubert is also commemorated with a monument in Stadtpark. It was commissioned by the men's choir Wiener Männergesangsverein, and was created by Carl Kundmann in 1872.

4 Memorial against War and Fascism

MAP M5 ■ Albertinaplatz/ Augustinerstrasse 8

The Austrian sculptor Alfred Hrdlicka created a monument in 1988–91 to commemorate all those killed during the National Socialist regime and World War II. Separate elements, made of granite from the area of the Mauthausen concentration camp, are arranged on the square where the Philipphof house was situated. The house was destroyed during an air raid on 12 March 1945 and more than 300 people were buried alive in its debris. The Proclamation of the Second Austrian Republic is carved on the "Stone of the Republic" here.

5 Mariensäule Am Hof

MAP M2 ■ Am Hof

Am Hof is dominated by a monument to the Virgin Mary (1664–7) that was cast in bronze by Balthasar Herold. The base shows four angels fighting with four animals, which are symbolic of the four major catastrophes for humankind in the 17th century. The dragon stands for starvation, the lion for war, the fantastical basilisk for the plague, while a snake represents the catastrophe of heresy.

6 Goethe Monument

MAP L5 ■ Opernring/ Goethegasse

Next to the Burggarten is a large monument to one of the greatest writers in the German language, Johann Wolfgang von Goethe. The statue *(see p116)*, seated on a massive base and cast in bronze, was created by Austrian sculptor Edmund von Hellmer in 1900. Also nearby is a memorial statue to another distinguished German writer and Goethe's contemporary, Friedrich Schiller.

Goethe Monument

The Maria Theresa Monument in front of the Naturhistorisches Museum

⑦ Maria Theresa Monument

MAP K5 ■ Maria-Theresien-Platz

Between the Kunsthistorisches and Naturhistorisches museums is a statue of Empress Maria Theresa (1717–80). The famed German sculptor Kaspar von Zumbusch created this elaborate monument in 1888, presenting the empress seated on the throne surrounded by ministers and advisors, as well as composers such as Mozart and Haydn.

⑧ Klimt's Grave

Hietzinger Friedhof, Maxingstrasse 15 ■ U-Bahn U4

The grave of the leading Secessionist artist Gustav Klimt (see p31) is found in the Hietzinger Cemetery, located close to Schloss Schönbrunn. Klimt's simple gravestone bears his name in the way he signed his works of art. He died in the year 1918 following a stroke.

⑨ Schönberg's Grave

Zentralfriedhof, Simmeringer Hauptstrasse 234 ■ Tram 71

The composer Arnold Schönberg (1874–1951),

creator of the 12-tone serial music technique (see p61), has a striking modern cube as his gravestone. It was designed by the Austrian sculptor Fritz Wotruba.

⑩ Mahler's Grave

Grinzinger Friedhof, An den langen Lüssen 33 ■ Train Grinzing

Gustav Mahler, director of the Vienna State Opera from 1897 to 1907, was buried at the Grinzinger Friedhof in 1911. The cemetery is in a peaceful location on the outskirts of the city. Mahler's simple white gravestone was designed by his friend, the architect and designer Josef Hoffmann.

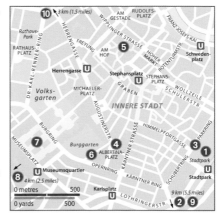

Museums

Fascinating aircrafts on display at the Technisches Museum Wien

① Technisches Museum Wien

Mariahilfer Strasse 212 ■ U-Bahn Schönbrunn; Tram 52, 60 ■ Open 9am–6pm Mon–Fri, 10am–6pm Sat & Sun ■ Adm (under 19s free) ■ www.technischesmuseum.at

Opened in 1918, this museum houses more than 80,000 exhibits relating to technology, energy and heavy industry.

② Camera and Photography Museum Westlicht

MAP E1 ■ Westbahnstrasse 40 ■ Tram 5, 49 ■ Open 11am–7pm daily (until 9pm Thu) ■ Adm ■ www.westlicht.com

Around 800 cameras are on display, including KGB spy cameras disguised as cigarette packets or evening bags.

③ Dom Museum Wien

MAP N3 ■ Stephansplatz 6 ■ U-Bahn 1, 3 ■ Open 10am–6pm Wed–Sun (until 8pm Thu) ■ Adm ■ www.dommuseum.at

Located in the Archbishop's Palace, this museum displays religious art, including 9th-century manuscripts.

④ Mozarthaus Vienna

MAP N3 ■ Domgasse 5 ■ U-Bahn 1, 3 ■ Open 10am–7pm daily ■ Adm ■ www.mozarthaus vienna.at

Mozart occupied a flat on the first floor of the Figarohaus in 1784–7.

He composed some of his greatest symphonies here *(see p61)*, including *The Marriage of Figaro*. The museum has exhibitions as well as Mozart's first-floor flat.

⑤ Museum für angewandte Kunst (MAK)

MAP Q3 ■ Stubenring 5 ■ U-Bahn 3; Tram 2 ■ Open 10am–6pm Tue–Sun (until 10pm Tue) ■ Adm (under 19s free) ■ www.mak.at

The Austrian Museum of Applied Arts includes world-famous works by the Wiener Werkstätte, an arts and crafts studio from 1870 to 1956.

⑥ Naturhistorisches Museum

Especially enthralling for children and their parents, the fascinating Natural History Museum *(see p107)* is world-class, both for its curious collection, as well as its architecture.

Exhibits at Naturhistorisches Museum

7 Heeresgeschichtliches
Arsenal, Objekt 18 ■ Bus 69A, 13A; Tram O, D, 18 ■ Open 9am–5pm daily ■ Adm (under 19s and first Sun of month free) ■ www.hgm.or.at
The Museum of Military History documents the imperial army from the 16th century to 1918.

8 Jüdisches Museum der Stadt Wien
MAP M4 ■ Palais Eskeles, Dorotheer-gasse 11 ■ U-Bahn 1, 3 ■ Open 10am–6pm Sun–Fri (closed Jewish hols) ■ Adm (under 18s free) ■ www.jmw.at
The world's first Jewish museum was founded in Vienna in 1895, but its exhibits were confiscated by National Socialists in 1938. The present museum, housed inside the Palais Eskeles, has a library as well as archives. Nearby, another museum, at Judenplatz, displays excavations of a medieval synagogue.

Stairwell in the Haus der Musik

9 Haus der Musik
MAP N5 ■ Seilerstätte 30 ■ Tram 2 ■ Open 10am–10pm daily ■ Adm ■ www.hdm.at
At the House of Music visitors are invited to experiment with sounds, to play giant instruments or to "conduct" the Vienna Philharmonic Orchestra.

10 Wien Museum Karlsplatz
MAP F5 ■ Karlsplatz ■ U-Bahn 1, 2, 4 ■ Open 10am–6pm Tue–Sun & public hols ■ Adm (under 19s and first Sun of month free) ■ Free guided tours ■ www.wienmuseum.at
Set over three storeys, this museum documents the history of Vienna with items spanning 7,000 years.

TOP 10 UNUSUAL MUSEUMS

Exhibits at the Clownmuseum

1 Clownmuseum
Ilgplatz 7
A collection of colourful circus posters, props, costumes and programmes.

2 Fiakermuseum
Veronikagasse 12
A museum dedicated to the Viennese horse-drawn carriages known as *fiaker*.

3 Kriminalmuseum
MAP B5 ■ Grosse Sperlgasse 24
Shows the city's most sensational crimes, from the Middle Ages to the present.

4 Schnapsmuseum
Wilhelmstrasse 19–21
Set in an old distillery, this museum is devoted to the Austrian drink, schnapps.

5 Uhrenmuseum
MAP M2 ■ Schulhof 2
Timepieces of all ages and shapes.

6 Josephinum
A collection of anatomical wax models once used to train surgeons (see p102).

7 Pathologisch-Anatomisches Museum
MAP B2 ■ Vienna University Campus, Spitalgasse 2
A former psychiatric ward houses a morbid collection of medical horrors.

8 Third Man Museum
MAP F3 ■ Pressgasse 25
A museum dedicated to the 1949 classic movie *The Third Man*, filmed in Vienna.

9 Bestattungsmuseum
This undertakers' museum (see p67) in Vienna's Zentralfriedhof (Central Cemetery) displays a variety of funereal objects.

10 Kaffeemuseum
MAP H3 ■ Vogelsanggasse 36, A-10
This small museum celebrates coffee, the favourite drink of the Viennese.

🔟 Art Galleries

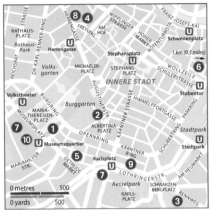

1 Kunsthistorisches Museum

The impressive imperial art collection is housed in the Kunsthistorisches Museum *(see pp22–5)* and includes one of the world's finest gatherings of works by the Old Masters.

Interior of the Albertina palace

2 Albertina

The Albertina palace *(see p91)* houses a collection of graphic art, architectural drawings and photographs from all periods. The 65,000 drawings and almost a million prints include works by Dürer and Klimt.

3 The Belvedere

This Baroque palace *(see pp28–31)* is home to a wonderful collection of Austrian artworks, including paintings by Gustav Klimt and Egon Schiele. The Upper Belvedere displays art from the Middle Ages onwards while the Lower Belvedere houses temporary exhibitions.

4 Kunstforum Bank Austria

MAP L2 ▪ Freyung 8
▪ Open 10am–6pm daily
▪ Adm ▪ www.kunstforum wien.at

Dedicated to the modern classics and their forerunners, the Kunstforum organizes several major exhibitions a year. By presenting shows of world-famous artists such as Egon Schiele, Oskar Kokoschka, Paul Cézanne, Pablo Picasso and Vincent van Gogh, the gallery is a magnet for visitors and has always attracted large crowds of art lovers.

5 Akademie der bildenden Künste Art Collections

The Academy of Fine Arts Vienna *(see p115)* possesses outstanding collections of old masters (Painting Gallery), as well as prints and drawings (Graphic Collection). Regular special exhibitions show selected works along with contemporary art.

6 KunstHaus Wien

Untere Weissgerberstrasse 13
▪ Open 10am–6pm daily ▪ Adm
▪ www.kunsthauswien.com

The only permanent collection of the works of Austrian artist Friedensreich Hundertwasser, whose passion for the irregular was largely inspired by Viennese Secessionists, is housed in this privately funded gallery. Located near the famous Hundertwasserhaus *(see pp40–41)*, KunstHaus welcomes close to 200,000 visitors a year. The museum's black-and-white façade, uneven floors and roof gardens were designed by the artist himself in 1989.

MuseumsQuartier, a Kunsthalle venue

The abbey's stunning treasures include tapestries, furniture and many liturgical objects. Most important of all are the museum's religious landscape and portrait paintings from all periods.

⑦ Kunsthalle
MAP J5 & MAP F4 ▪ Museumsplatz 1 & Treitlstrasse 2 ▪ Open 11am–7pm Tue–Sun (until 9pm Thu) ▪ Adm ▪ www.kunsthallewien.at

Specializing in contemporary art, the Kunsthalle has two venues – one within the MuseumsQuartier (see p34) and the other at Karlsplatz – enabling its curators to feature several fascinating changing exhibitions. At the Karlsplatz site, the exhibits can be seen from the outside, as the building is made entirely of glass.

⑧ Museum im Schottenstift
MAP L2 ▪ Freyung 6 ▪ Open 11am–5pm Tue–Fri (until 4:30pm Sat; closed public hols) ▪ Adm ▪ www. schotten.wien

The Scots' Abbey, founded in 1155 by Scottish and Irish Benedictine monks, is a massive complex, containing a church, a school and a monastery.

⑨ Albertina Modern
MAP N6 ▪ Karlsplatz 5 ▪ www.albertina.at

Located in the Künstlerhaus building, the Albertina Modern houses a vast collection of modern and contemporary art. There are over four temporary exhibitions a year on subjects like graphic art and photography. Past exhibitions have included works by Jackson Pollock, Joan Mitchell, Ai Weiwei and Valie Export.

⑩ mumok
This gallery is officially named the Museum Moderner Kunst Stiftung Ludwig Wien (see p34). It contains one of the largest European collections of modern and contemporary art, from American Pop Art, Photo Realism, Fluxus and Nouveau Réalism to Viennese Actionism, Arte Povera, Conceptual and Minimal Art. The galleries are split chronologically over five levels, two underground. Tours in English are held at 4pm on Saturdays.

mumok, MuseumsQuartier

🔟 Composers

① Joseph Haydn

Along with Beethoven and Mozart, Haydn (1732–1809) is the third important composer of the Vienna Classical period (1750–1830). He moved to Vienna aged eight, to become a choirboy at Stephansdom. In his house at Haydngasse 19 he wrote his greatest works, such as the oratorio *The Creation* (1796–8).

② Wolfgang Amadeus Mozart

Although born in Salzburg, the life of this world-famous composer (1756–91) is inextricably intertwined with Vienna. Mozart moved to the city in 1781 after falling out with his sponsor, the Archbishop of Salzburg. It was here that he wrote his greatest works and celebrated all his triumphs and misfortunes until he died, aged 35.

Portrait of Franz Schubert

Manuscript handwritten by Mozart

③ Ludwig van Beethoven

When Ludwig van Beethoven (1770–1827) gave his first concert in the Vienna Court Theatre in 1795 he already had a reputation as an excellent pianist. Born in Bonn, he moved to Vienna aged 22 to receive tuition from Joseph Haydn and, briefly, Mozart. In 1805 his opera *Fidelio* premiered at the Theater an der Wien (see p116).

Gilded statue of Johann Strauss

④ Franz Schubert

The twelfth child born in the family home at Nussdorfer Strasse 54, in Vienna, Franz Schubert (1797–1828) composed many symphonies, although it is for his songs that he is best remembered.

⑤ Anton Bruckner

Born in a village in Upper Austria, Bruckner (1824–96) moved to the capital in 1868, when he became a professor at the city's musical academy. Well respected today, his contemporaries were critical about his music and some of his pieces were never performed during his lifetime.

⑥ Johann Strauss II

Vienna's "Waltz King" (1825–99) was the most successful of a dynasty of composers and musicians. He wrote more than 500 dance pieces, among them the *Blue Danube Waltz* (1867), which became Austria's unofficial national anthem. Strauss is buried at the Zentralfriedhof (see p127).

7 Johannes Brahms

Born in Hamburg in 1833, Brahms became the musical director of the Vienna Singakademie, a choral society, in 1862. For three seasons he directed the Vienna Philharmonic Orchestra, but from 1878 onwards he devoted all of his time to composition. Brahms died in 1897 and is also buried at the Zentralfriedhof.

8 Gustav Mahler

Renowned conductor and composer, Mahler (1860–1911) wrote ten symphonies and song cycles in his life. He was the musical director of the court opera (1897–1907) and led the opera into its golden age. His compositions, including the beautiful *Symphony No. 5*, are some of the most frequently performed works.

Photograph of Gustav Mahler

9 Arnold Schönberg

Founder of the 12-tone serial technique, Schönberg (1874–1951) became one of the 20th century's most renowned composers. He left Vienna in 1933 in the wake of National Socialism and died in the US.

10 Olga Neuwirth

Born in 1968, Neuwirth is an Austrian composer, visual artist and author. Her operas, such as *Orlando*, based on a novel by Virginia Woolf, are often influenced by literary works. She has also collaborated with her partner, the writer Elfriede Jelinek.

TOP 10 MOZART'S VIENNA

1 Mozartplatz
MAP G4
Characters from the opera *The Magic Flute* watch over the square (*see p65*).

2 Tiefer Graben
MAP M2
Mozart stayed at the house at No. 18 on this street during his first concert tour to Vienna in 1762.

3 Palais Collalto
MAP M2 ▪ Am Hof 13
The six-year-old Mozart gave his first Vienna concert here in 1762.

4 Griechenbeisl
MAP P2 ▪ Fleischmarkt 11
On one of the walls in Vienna's oldest inn you will find Mozart's signature among those of other famous visitors.

5 Stephansdom
Mozart married Constanze Weber on 4 August 1782 in Vienna's impressive cathedral (*see pp12–15*).

6 Café Frauenhuber
MAP N4 ▪ Himmelpfortgasse 6
Mozart gave piano concerts in the music room of the café.

7 Mozart's Piano
MAP L4 ▪ Neue Burg ▪ Adm
Instruments believed to have been played by Mozart are housed in the Sammlung alter Musikinstrumente.

8 Mozart's Grave
Mozart was buried at St Marx Cemetery (*see p130*) but the site of his actual grave remains unknown.

9 Mozart Cenotaph
Simmeringer Hauptstrasse
A cenotaph commemorating Mozart was relocated from St Marx Cemetery to the Zentralfriedhof in 1891.

10 Mozarthaus Vienna
Mozart wrote his most famous opera, *The Marriage of Figaro*, here (*see p56*).

Exterior of the Mozarthaus

🔟 Underground Vienna

The Third Man **sewer tour**

1 Sewers
3. Mann Tour: MAP M6; Karlsplatz-Girardipark (U1, U2, U4), opposite the Café Museum; tours May–Oct: 10am–8pm Thu–Sun on the hour; adm; www.drittemanntour.at

Vienna's sewers came to fame in the 1949 film classic *The Third Man*, when Harry Lime, played by Orson Welles, was chased through the city's underworld by the police. Filmed in postwar Vienna, the movie is still remembered today, as several tours follow in the characters' footsteps, taking visitors through the several iconic filming locations.

2 Römermuseum
MAP D4 ■ Hoher Markt 3 ■ Open 9am–6pm Tue–Sun ■ Adm

Remains of the ancient Roman camp Vindobona *(see p48)* can be seen at

Exhibits at the Römermuseum

this superb underground museum. Excavations show archaeological finds such as pottery and coins.

3 Michaelerkirche Crypt
Well-preserved mummies, some still wearing Baroque frocks and wigs, are preserved in this crypt *(see p51)*. From 1631 to 1784, some 4,000 bodies were buried here, including nobles who wanted to rest close to the emperor at Hofburg.

4 Kunst im Prückel
MAP Q3 ■ Biberstrasse 2 ■ 01 512 54 00 ■ Open 8:30am–10pm daily

Hidden away in the basement of the popular vintage coffee house Café Prückel *(see p98)* is this tiny gem of a venue. An eclectic theatre staging intimate drama, cabaret, concerts and literary soirées, it lends a quirky, magical vibe to the neighbourhood.

5 Stephansdom Catacombs
In the 18th century many graveyards across Europe were closed down as plague epidemics spread quickly in the cities. Some cemeteries were relocated beneath city churches, and people's bones were reburied in the crypts. The catacombs *(see p13)* under the Gothic Stephansdom were built after Emperor Charles VI shut down the cathedral's graveyard in 1732. They are filled with the bones of

some 11,000 people. Today it is hard to imagine that the Stephansplatz was once crammed with gravestones.

6 Virgilkapelle
MAP N3 ■ Stephansplatz U-Bahn station ■ Open 10am–6pm Tue–Sun ■ Adm ■ www.wienmuseum.at

The large Gothic St Virgil's Chapel was only discovered in the 1970s, when the metro line U1 was built – it had been hidden underground for some 200 years. Established in the 1200s, it was used for public burials until a Vienna merchant turned it into his private crypt in the 14th century.

7 Cabaret Fledermaus
MAP M3 ■ Spiegelgasse 2 ■ Open 9pm–6am Wed–Mon ■ Adm

A long staircase leads down to the Cabaret Fledermaus, named after the bats (Fledermäuse) that inhabited Vienna's cellars in the Middle Ages. The venue plays retro music, but there are also themed nights featuring other genres, some with free admission.

8 Augustinerkirche
MAP M4 ■ Augustinerstrasse 3 (entrance on Josefsplatz) ■ Open 8am–6pm daily ■ Adm

St Augustin's Church, built in 1327 in Gothic style, hosted many imperial weddings but the church is most famous for its Herzgruft (hearts' crypt) containing the hearts of Austria's emperors.

9 Kapuzinergruft
MAP M4 ■ Tegetthoffstrasse 2 ■ Open 10am–6pm daily ■ Adm

The crypt underneath the Kapuzinerkirche (Capuchin Church) was built by Empress Anna in 1618 and served as the burial place of the Habsburgs for over 350 years. Among the 140 elite bodies resting here are 12 emperors

Habsburg tomb, Kapuzinergruft crypt

and 19 empresses. However, their hearts were removed and buried in silver containers in the crypt of Augustinerkirche and their intestines in copper urns in the catacombs of Stephansdom.

10 Wine Cellars
In the Middle Ages, most Vienna houses had as many storeys below ground as they had above. The cellars stored wine, vegetables and other goods. This underground labyrinth was often connected by tunnels. Some cellars continue to exist today as "Keller" restaurants. These include the Rathauskeller at Wipplingerstrasse 8 and the Esterhazykeller at Haarhof 1.

TOP 10 Parks and Gardens

1 Stadtpark
MAP P5 ■ Parkring

Vienna's oldest public park, bisected by the River Wien, was designed as an artificial landscape in 1862, with paths winding through grassy areas, past ponds and beautiful shrubs and flowers. Stadtpark is most famous, however, for the statue (see p54) of the "King of Waltz", Johann Strauss.

2 Augarten
MAP A5 ■ Obere Augarten-strasse 1

An oasis of style and serenity, Vienna's oldest Baroque park has been open to the public since 1775. Within this pretty, leafy park lies the excellent Augarten Porcelain Manufactory and Museum (see p66) and a World War II-era anti-aircraft tower.

3 Burggarten
MAP L5 ■ Josefsplatz 1

Behind the National Library is the pretty Burggarten, landscaped in the formal English style and usually inhabited by sun-worshippers on summer days. Located in the Art Nouveau greenhouse, built in 1901, is a stylish café-bar and restaurant.

4 Schönbrunn Park
The beautiful grounds of the Schloss Schönbrunn (see pp42–5) include ponds, fountains and a maze.

Stunning Schönbrunn Park

The Volksgarten in full bloom

5 Volksgarten
MAP K3

This garden, between the Burgtheater and Heldenplatz, is popular with students from the nearby university and office workers on their lunch breaks. Its beautiful rose beds bloom spectacularly in spring. The replica of the Temple of Theseus in Athens is used for a range of changing exhibitions.

6 Prater
Prater, 1020

A former 18th-century imperial hunting ground, the Wurstelprater – known as the Prater (see p85) – is a large public park today. In 2016 it celebrated 250 years of public access. Leafy walks, fairground rides, food stalls, a Ferris wheel and two racecourses are among its highlights.

7 Alpengarten im Belvedere

Established in 1803 by the Habsburg Archduke Johann, this is Europe's oldest alpine garden and is part of the Belvedere park *(see pp28–9)*. The tiny wild garden, beside the more formal Belvedere gardens, is home to more than 4,000 plants, among them a bonsai collection.

8 Rathauspark
MAP K2

The park in front of the town hall is busy year round with various festivals, ranging from a Christmas market and ice rink in winter to a summer film and music festival. Many monuments and fountains complement the layout of the park. Another attraction is the large number of centuries-old trees.

9 Tiroler Garten
Schloss Schönbrunn

Archduke Johann so admired the Tyrolean landscape and architecture that he ordered that an area within Schönbrunn Park be kept as a natural alpine landscape in the 19th century. Today it has an alpine-style house with a small farm and an orchard.

10 Sigmund Freud Park

The green area stretching from Vienna University to the Votivkirche is usually packed with students and picnickers on warm summer days. In the park *(see p104)*, a ring of different trees surrounding a granite table and chairs represents the member states of the European Union.

TOP 10 FOUNTAINS

The Neptunbrunnen fountain

1 Neptunbrunnen
Neptune overlooks cascades at Schönbrunn Palace *(see pp42–5)*.

2 Mozartbrunnen
MAP F4 ▪ Mozartplatz
This delicate Jugendstil fountain depicts scenes from the opera *The Magic Flute*.

3 Hochstrahlbrunnen
MAP F5 ▪ Schwarzenbergplatz
The enormous fountain, floodlit on summer nights, was built in 1873.

4 Vermählungsbrunnen
MAP N2 ▪ Hoher Markt
Josef Emanuel von Erlach built this fountain of marble and bronze in 1732.

5 Andromedabrunnen
MAP M2 ▪ Old Town Hall, Wipplingerstrasse 8
Sculpted by Georg Raphael Donner in 1741, this fountain, shows Andromeda in the fangs of a sea monster.

6 Pallas Athene Brunnen
MAP K3 ▪ Dr-Karl-Renner-Ring 3
A statue of the Greek goddess of wisdom towers over the fountain.

7 Danubius Brunnen
MAP M5 ▪ Albertinaplatz
Part of the Albertina building, the fountain features stories of the Danube.

8 Michaelerplatz Brunnen
MAP L3
The monumental fountains of the Hofburg, Macht zu Lande and Macht zur See, can be seen at this square.

9 Schutzengelbrunnen
MAP F4 ▪ Rilkeplatz
Little dragons spout water beneath the angel who gives this fountain its name.

10 Yunus Emre Fountain
Türkenschanzpark ▪ Tram 41
A gift from the Turkish government, the fountain is decorated in gilt script and beautiful tiles.

🔟 Off the Beaten Track

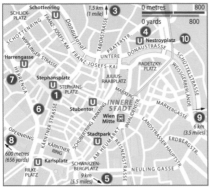

on secret courtyards, tall towers and the city's most unattractive buildings.

3 Augarten Porcelain Manufactory and Museum

MAP B6 ■ Obere Augartenstrasse 1 ■ U-Bahn U2 ■ Open 10am–5pm Mon–Sat; manufactory tours 11:30am Mon–Thu ■ www.augarten.com

This fascinating museum charts the history of Vienna porcelain, with exhibits from the imperial manufactory (1718–1866) and its successor Augarten (founded in 1923).

1 Stock im Eisen

MAP N3 ■ Corner of Graben and Kärntner Strasse, Stephansplatz

In the Middles Ages, trees were studded with nails for good luck – nails were valuable and the tree an offering to God. A 600-year-old section of such a tree is displayed behind glass on the corner of the striking Palais Equitable mansion.

2 Whoosh Vienna

www.whoosh.wien

This community-focused group celebrates modern Vienna in all its complexity. It offers various offbeat themed walking tours, including ones

Exhibits at Johann Strauss Apartment

4 Johann Strauss Apartment

MAP C6 ■ Praterstrasse 54 ■ U-Bahn U1 to Nestroyplatz ■ 01 214 01 21 ■ Open 10am–1pm, 2–6pm Tue–Sun & public hols

Located in the Leopoldstadt, this apartment was the home of Austrian composer Johann Strauss II from 1863 until 1870. This was where he composed, among other works, the famous *Blue Danube Waltz*, Austria's unofficial national anthem. Exhibits here include manuscripts, furniture and a valuable Amati violin.

Exhibits at the Bestattungsmuseum

5 Bestattungsmuseum
Simmeringer Hauptstrasse 234 ▪ Bus 106; Tram 71 ▪ 01 760 67 ▪ Open Mar–Nov: 9am–4:30pm Mon–Fri, 10am–5:30pm Sat; Dec–Feb: 9am–4:30pm Mon–Fri ▪ www. bestattungsmuseum.at

This unusual museum is testament to a proud Viennese funeral tradition. Housed in Europe's second-largest cemetery, it contains a macabre collection of coffins, pall-bearers' attire, skulls and other oddities that celebrate the business of death.

6 Elmayer Dance School
MAP M3 ▪ Bräunerstrasse 13 ▪ 01 512 71 97 ▪ Open 3–8pm daily (closed school hols) ▪ Adm ▪ www. elmayer.at/en

Book yourself a lesson at the Elmayer Dance School to master the Viennese waltz. Very soon, you'll be swirling around at 180 beats per minute after 50 minutes of professional tuition here. Call ahead for private lessons.

7 Globe Museum
MAP L2 ▪ Palais Mollard, Herrengasse 9 ▪ 01 534 10 700 ▪ Open Jun–Sep: 10am–6pm daily; Oct–May: 10am–6pm Tue–Sun (until 9pm Thu) ▪ Adm ▪ www.onb.ac.at

Among the fascinating collections of worldly exhibits in Vienna is the Globe Museum – said to be the only museum in the world singularly devoted to globes. Marvel at more than 600 terrestrial and celestial globular maps – some as large as an adult.

8 Damage Unlimited
MAP G3 ▪ Mariahilfer Strasse 23–25 ▪ 0676 668 18 61 ▪ Open 11am–7pm Mon–Sat ▪ www.damage-town.com

Considered Vienna's answer to Comic-Con, Damage Unlimited is where you can play old-fashioned board games or electronic first-person shooters. Look out for the cosplay (costume play) crowd.

9 Summer Beaches
Open May–Sep daily

Few visitors know that Vienna has a fine collection of beaches. For some downtime on the city's artificial sandbanks simply bring a picnic, sunscreen and a swimsuit to one of the half a dozen different venues along the Donaukanal.

Relaxing on one of Vienna's beaches

10 Republic of Kugelmugel
Antifaschismusplatz 2, Wiener Prater ▪ U-Bahn U2

No need for a passport to visit this self-proclaimed sovereign micro-nation – an unusual ball-shaped house located in Prater park (see p85). The house was built by Austrian artist Edwin Lipburger in 1971 and the Republic status declared in 1976 after Lipburger fell out with the authorities over building permits. He even printed his own stamps.

TOP 10 Children's Attractions

Exhibit of a scene from Mozart's *The Magic Flute* at the Marionettentheater

1 Marionettentheater Schönbrunn

Hofratstrakt, Schloss Schönbrunn
■ U-Bahn 4 Schönbrunn ■ 01 817 32 47 ■ Adm ■ www.marionetten theater.at

The puppet theatre in the little court theatre at Schönbrunn stages wonderful shows that delight children and adults alike. A version of Mozart's *The Magic Flute* is the undisputed highlight of the programme, with a feather-clad Tamino and a fantastic vicious snake.

Children at the Technisches Museum

2 Technisches Museum Wien

A special adventure area at Vienna's Museum of Technology *(see p56)* is geared towards children aged two to eight years old (although older kids enjoy it too) and allows young visitors to actively engage with the technical sciences behind road, maritime and air transport, as well as space exploration. The museum also features a full calendar of events and free-of-charge workshops in the museum's kindergarten. The "crazy laboratory" workshops are highly sought-after.

3 Haus des Meeres

MAP F2 ■ Esterhazypark ■ 01 587 14 17 ■ Open 9am–6pm daily (until 9pm Thu) ■ Adm ■ www.haus-des-meeres.at

Fish and reptiles from all across the world have found a home in a former anti-aircraft tower in Esterhazypark. You can "journey" from the chilly North Sea to the Australian Great Barrier Reef, taking in the natural landscape en route. Very popular with kids are the sharks' and piranhas' feeding time in the "Amazon pool".

4 Hütteldorfer Bad

Linzer Strasse 376 ■ U-Bahn 4 Hütteldorf ■ 01 416 38 20 ■ Open 8am–9pm daily ■ www.wien.gv.at/freizeit/hallenbaeder

This municipal swimming pool offers many attractions for children, such as adventure streams, slides and water cannons. A large outdoor play area is open during summer months.

5 Schloss Schönbrunn

Young visitors are given a glimpse of imperial life in the palace from a child's perspective at the Children's Museum (see p43). In the Court Bakery they can watch confectioners make cakes and pastries – which can be sampled fresh from the oven.

6 Schönbrunn Zoo

Considered the oldest zoo (see p45) in the world, this has all the usual favourites, including elephants, reptiles and butterflies. Most are housed in Baroque-style compounds.

7 Schmetterlinghaus

MAP L5 ▪ Burggarten, Burgring ▪ Open Apr–Oct: 10am–4:45pm Mon–Fri, 10am–6:15pm Sat, Sun & public hols; Nov–Mar: 10am–3:45pm daily ▪ Adm ▪ www.schmetterlinghaus.at

This large Art Nouveau greenhouse contains more than 150 species of tropical butterflies and moths, living in microclimatic habitats that replicate their natural environment.

8 Schönbrunn Park

This beautiful park (see p45) is home to two special attractions – the maze and the labyrinth. The maze is based on the original 18th-century designs and its tracks through the hedges lead to a wonderful viewing platform in the middle that overlooks the area. The labyrinth is a games zone featuring a giant kaleidoscope, a climbing pole and fun riddles.

9 Riesenrad

Prater 90 ▪ U-Bahn Praterstern ▪ 01 729 54 30 ▪ Open May–Aug: 9am–midnight daily; Sep–Apr: times vary, check website for details ▪ Adm ▪ www.wienerriesenrad.com

Over 100 years old, Vienna's giant Ferris wheel at the Prater (see p64) offers fantastic views over the city's rooftops. Be sure to visit the small museum in the entrance area, where the history of the wheel and the city are told in some of the Riesenrad's old red cabins.

Getting creative at ZOOM

10 ZOOM

Designed exclusively for children, ZOOM is a place of playful enquiry, learning and discovery. Hands-on exhibitions for toddlers, kitchens for cooking experiments and the chance to "zoom" in on new situations and learn about the world are just some of the highlights at this interactive museum (see p35). Booking ahead is recommended.

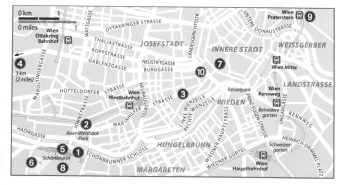

🔟 Theatres

The Volkstheater's sumptuous interior

1 Volkstheater
Since it was built in 1889, the historic Volkstheater, or People's Theatre (see p107), has always aimed at making modern and classic literature accessible to a broader audience. With nearly 1,000 seats, this is among the largest theatres in the German-speaking world.

2 Rabenhof
Rabengasse 3 ■ U-Bahn U3 ■ www.rabenhoftheater.com
In the 1920s, the Rabenhof was constructed as council housing for workers, and an assembly hall catering to the workers' union was built in the basement. The structure was adapted to become a theatre between 1987 and 1992. Today, the theatre's repertoire includes modern plays, comedies and other performances.

3 Akademietheater
MAP P6 ■ Lisztstrasse 1 ■ www.burgtheater.at
The Akademietheater is part of the Konzerthaus building (see p73). It initially functioned as the training stage for the nearby Academy of Music and Performing Arts, but in 1922 it became the "small" venue for the Burgtheater ensemble. Mainly classic modern plays are staged here.

4 Kasino am Schwarzenbergplatz
MAP F5 ■ Schwarzenbergplatz 1 ■ www.burgtheater.at
This is an intimate stage, located in a former officers' mess of the imperial army that was adapted as a venue in the 1990s. Its extensive programme includes contemporary plays, often followed by talks with the actors.

5 Raimund Theater
Wallgasse 18–20 ■ U-Bahn U6 ■ www.musicalvienna.at
Named after Austrian playwright and actor Ferdinand Raimund, this theatre opened with one of his plays in 1893. After a period of staging operettas, the theatre was renovated and modernized. It now hosts musical theatre performances.

Performance at the Raimund Theater

6 Theater in der Josefstadt
MAP D2 ■ Josefstädter Strasse 26 ■ www.josefstadt.org
Built in 1788 following the design of Josef Kornhäusel, this theatre was entirely rebuilt in 1822 and reopened with a musical piece by Beethoven, composed for the occasion.

7 Kammerspiele
MAP P2
■ Rotenturmstrasse 20
■ www.josefstadt.org

This 515-seat theatre was built in the year 1910. Initially known as the Residenztheater, it is closely connected to the Theater in der Josefstadt and actors usually perform in different plays in both venues. The Kammerspiele's programme is made up entirely of comedies.

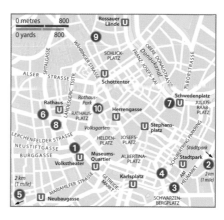

8 Vienna's English Theatre
MAP D2 ■ Josefsgasse 12
■ www.englishtheatre.at

Vienna's English Theatre was founded in 1963 and is the oldest English-language theatre in continental Europe. It was initially intended as a summer venue for tourists but soon extended its programme to run all year round. The stage has attracted world stars such as Anthony Quinn and Judi Dench to its successful productions.

9 Schauspielhaus
MAP B3 ■ Porzellangasse 19
■ www.schauspielhaus.at

The Schauspielhaus is a venue that offers a multifaceted programme, including literary readings and light operas as well as contemporary drama. Since its foundation in 1978, the theatre has hosted not only many Austrian but also several world premieres, particularly by the Hungarian-born dramatist George Tabori (1914–2007). It is also one of the several venues for productions staged by the Wiener Festwochen, Vienna's most important theatre festival (see p86). Being fairly small, it gives the audience the advantage of being very close to the actors during the performances.

10 Burgtheater
The Burgtheater, or the imperial Court Theatre (see p93), is one of the most important theatres in the German-speaking world, and the choice of its director at any given period always arouses much political and cultural passion. Premieres of traditional as well as modern plays are closely scrutinized by the public, triggering either enthusiastic or dismissive reactions.

Vienna's Burgtheater

🔟 Music Venues

Gala concert performance in the Golden Hall at Vienna's Musikverein

1 Theater an der Wien

Having been a musical venue for many years, this stunning historic theatre (see p116) is once again a working opera house.

2 Ronacher

MAP N4 ▪ Seilerstätte 9
▪ www.musicalvienna.at

The original Ronacher, built in 1870, staged tragedies and comedies, but after it burned down in the 1880s architects Ferdinand Fellner and Hermann Helmer replaced it with a variety theatre. Neglected after World War II, the Ronacher reopened in 1988 with the hit musical *Cats*.

3 Musikverein

Public concert life began in Vienna with the foundation of the Society of Friends of Music in 1812. Up until then, musical concerts were restricted to aristocratic homes. This massive concert hall (see p121) was commissioned by the society in 1869 after previous locations had become too small. The society's aim was, and still is, to promote all music, and until 1909, it also ran a music academy with skilled teachers including Anton Bruckner and eminent students such as Gustav Mahler (see p61). This institution was the predecessor of the present Academy of Music.

4 RadioKulturhaus

MAP G5 ▪ Argentinierstrasse 30a ▪ www.radiokulturhaus.orf.at

The RadioKulturhaus offers a programme of jazz and classical concerts, literary readings and films. Most of the concerts are broadcast on the radio station Ö1.

5 Porgy & Bess

MAP P4 ▪ Riemergasse 11
▪ www.porgy.at

One of the top jazz clubs in town is mainly dedicated to modern jazz. Alongside star names, many newcomers also get the chance to play.

A performance of *Cats* at Ronacher

6 Jazzland

This traditional jazz club (see p97), founded in 1972, has a history of distinguished international and national artists performing in its cellar venue. It also hosts notable acts during the annual JazzFloor festival.

7 Volksoper

**MAP A2 ■ Währinger Strasse 78
■ www.volksoper.at**

The "People's Opera" opened in 1898 after a group of industrialists raised funds to celebrate Franz Joseph's Golden Jubilee. The theatre's façade has remained unchanged. Operettas and dances are performed here.

8 Staatsoper

In a city so intrinsically linked to classical music, no visitor should miss a tour of the spectacular State Opera House (see pp36–7).

Grand interior of the Staatsoper

9 Kammeroper

**MAP P2 ■ Fleischmarkt 24
■ www.theater-wien.at**

The Kammeroper, founded in 1954, is dedicated to promoting young singers. The five main productions a year include classic and Baroque operas, as well as some contemporary works.

10 Konzerthaus

**MAP P6 ■ Lothringerstrasse 20
www.konzerthaus.at**

The Vienna Concert House opened in 1913. Its design, by Ferdinand Fellner and Hermann Helmer, is clearly influenced by Art Nouveau style. With four concert halls, more than 3,100 seats, and a diverse programme, the venue attracts music lovers from all camps.

TOP 10 NIGHTCLUBS

Inside the Volksgarten nightclub

1 Volksgarten
Everything from tango to R&B nights is on offer here (see p97).

2 B72
**Hernalser Gürtelbogen 72–3
■ U-Bahn U6**
This trendy club in the arcades of the U6 metro plays electronic music.

3 U4
**Schönbrunner Strasse 222
■ U-Bahn U4**
Revel in theme nights ranging from boogie and hip-hop to classic rock.

4 Eden Bar
MAP N4 ■ Liliengasse 2
This tiny cellar bar is a popular meeting point for Vienna's high society.

5 Rhiz
U-Bahnbögen 37–8 ■ U-Bahn U6
Also in the arcades of the metro, Rhiz has a daily line-up of electronic music.

6 Flex
MAP B4 ■ Augartenbrücke
This underground club by the river has a lively indie and electronica scene.

7 Chelsea
Lerchenfelder Gürtel, U-Bahnbögen 29–30 ■ U-Bahn U6
Live bands and indie music are featured under the U6 metro line.

8 Qulture Club
MAP A2 ■ U-Bahn U6 ■ Untergrundbahnbögen 181–182
The perfect spot for hip-hop and urban tracks, with afro beats on Sundays.

9 Arena
Baumgasse 80 ■ Bus N75
Music here ranges from punk to indie.

10 Titanic
MAP F3 ■ U-Bahn U2 ■ Theobaldgasse 11
Spread over two floors, this club sounds electro, techno and old-style disco.

⓴ Viennese Dishes

① Zwiebelrostbraten
Slices of roast beef are topped with fried onion rings and served with mashed or roasted potatoes. A variation is *vanillerostbraten*, in which the meat is seasoned with garlic.

② Leberknödelsuppe
Austrians are fond of their soups and a traditional three-course Sunday lunch will often start off with a bowl of clear beef broth. This particular variety, served with little liver dumplings, is undoubtedly the best among Austrian soups.

③ Frankfurters
The takeaway sausage stall, or *würstelstand*, is found all over Vienna. Slim, pale sausages were introduced to Vienna in 1798 by the butcher Johann Georg Lahner, who named them after the city of Frankfurt, where they originated. They are usually served with mustard and a *semmel* (bread roll).

④ Frittatensuppe
Most soups are made of clear beef stock and are served with a range of garnishes to create some variety. Adding *frittaten* – pancakes seasoned with a sprinkle of fresh herbs, cut into thin strips and served in bouillon – is a popular option.

Tafelspitz, **Franz Joseph's favourite**

⑤ Tafelspitz
Meat is essential to Viennese cuisine, and beef has played a significant role throughout the centuries. The favourite among the many variations is *tafelspitz* – boiled rump, usually served with *rösti* (fried grated potatoes) or boiled potatoes and apple and horseradish sauce. Emperor Franz Joseph allegedly ate it every single day.

Tasty breaded *Weiner schnitzel*

⑥ Wiener Schnitzel
The roots of the *Wiener schnitzel* lie in ancient Byzantium, where meat was purportedly eaten after being sprinkled with gold. Over the course of time the precious metal was replaced by a coat of golden breadcrumbs. Count Radetzky, who fought several wars for the Austrian Empire in the 19th century, is said to have brought the dish to imperial Vienna from Milan. The outcome is tasty veal or pork covered in breadcrumbs and fried until golden. The classic side dish is potato salad.

⑦ Schweinsbraten mit Semmelknödel
Roast pork is another standard of Viennese cuisine. It is variously seasoned with flavours ranging from garlic to fresh herbs and caraway, and the meat is generally served with dumplings, salad and gravy.

A bowl of *Frittatensuppe*

8 Gefüllte Paprika
Stuffed peppers are a remnant of the Austro-Hungarian monarchy, when Vienna hosted people from all over Europe. Originally from the Balkans, the dish soon became popular across the city. Green peppers are stuffed with minced meat and rice and usually served with a tomato sauce.

9 Knödel
Vienna's many dumpling types, both sweet and savoury, include plain *knödel* with vegetables and meat, *germknödel* (dumpling with sour prune jam), *zwetschgenknödel* (plum dumpling), *topfenknödel* (curd cheese dumpling) and *griessnockerl* (semolina dumpling).

Zwetschgenknödeln **(plum dumplings)**

10 Gulasch
This dish is a successful marriage of Austrian and Hungarian cuisines. The original Hungarian soup-like dish arrived in Viennese kitchens and evolved into goulash – a spicy beef stew, seasoned with paprika and served with dumplings or bread rolls. It can also come with potatoes or a fried egg and gherkins.

Beef
Gulasch

TOP 10 VIENNESE CAKES

Classic *Schwarzwälderkirschtorte*

1 Schwarzwälderkirschtorte
Black Forest Gateau is a rich chocolate cake with layers of sponge sandwiched together with cream and sour cherries.

2 Gugelhupf
With almonds, cocoa or chocolate icing, this cake is baked in a fluted ring mould and is named for its shape.

3 Apfelstrudel
Strudel is an Austrian staple. Very thin dough is sprinkled with apples, cinnamon, raisins and icing sugar.

4 Dobostorte
This cake features eight layers of light sponge joined together with chocolate cream and glazed on top with caramel.

5 Linzertorte
Named after the Austrian city of Linz, this almond pastry filled with jam has been popular for nearly 300 years.

6 Malakofftorte
Cream and sponge biscuits drenched in rum are set together and smothered in butter-cream icing.

7 Esterhazytorte
This cake is made with almond sponge layers filled with cream and covered with marbled brown-and-white icing.

8 Rehrücken
The name of this chocolate cake is inspired from its baking mould, which is shaped like the saddle of a deer. The sponge is usually filled with apricot jam.

9 Sachertorte
In 1832, Viennese confectioner Franz Sacher allegedly invented this rich cake, covered with apricot jam then coated with chocolate.

10 Cremeschnitte
This consists of two layers of crispy puff pastry filled with a thick layer of vanilla-flavoured whipped cream.

🔟 Cafés

1 Café Demel

This café *(see p98)*, part of which resembles a Rococo-period salon, is one of Vienna's most refined retreats for cake lovers. Opened in 1786, it had become a hot spot for the Viennese upper classes by the mid-19th century, even providing the beloved Empress Sisi with her favourite sweet violet sorbet.

2 Café Museum

Designed by the minimalist architect Adolf Loos in 1899, this café *(see p118)* reflects his anti-ornamental aesthetic, and was once the haunt of artists including Klimt and Schiele. Remodelled in the 1930s, it has since been returned to its original design.

3 Café Diglas

Established in 1923, the Diglas *(see p98)* has marble tables, wooden chairs and little window booths fitted with red velvet sofas. Ordering a piece of cake – slices are served with a small mountain of whipped cream – is highly recommended.

4 Café Europa

This café *(see p118)* has all the amenities of a traditional coffee house, but with modern furnishings and a cheerful informality. It is known for being open until 5am, providing both pastries and cooked meals around the clock. There's also an American-style cocktail bar.

The iconic Café Landtmann

5 Café Landtmann

Franz Landtmann opened his café *(see p98)* in 1873. Sigmund Freud used to have his morning coffee here, as did the artistic director of the Burgtheater, Max Reinhardt. Landtmann bustles with activity day and night – it has a large shaded terrace, and the four interior rooms are elegantly decorated with velvet upholstery, starched linen table-cloths, crystal light fixtures and large mirrors with inlaid wood.

6 Café Central

One of the city's best-known cafés, the Central *(see p98)* was the meeting place for Vienna's intellectuals at the turn of the 19th century – the poet Peter Altenberg gathered a literary circle and he even had his mail delivered here. Leon Trotsky was also one of the regulars during his Vienna exile prior to World War I. Today the Central serves almost 1,000 cups of coffee a day in its charming and elegant setting.

Enchanting interior of Café Central

7 Café Bräunerhof
This place *(see p98)* has a traditional living-room atmosphere, cosy but worn, thanks to a stream of customers dating back to the 1900s. It has always been a literary café – the writers Alfred Polgar and Hugo von Hofmannsthal were regulars.

8 Café Hawelka
Bustling Hawelka *(see p98)*, opened in the 1930s, has old-world charm. The owners often took paintings from artists in exchange for food. As a result the walls are covered with works by Ernst Fuchs, among others.

Café Hawelka's poster-covered walls

9 Café Prückel
Famous for its 1950s ambience, this café *(see p98)* hosts music and plays in its basement.

10 Café Sperl
Built in grand style in 1880, Sperl *(see p118)* has long been a haunt of artists and musicians from the nearby Theater an der Wien. It hosts live piano music every Sunday afternoon from September to June.

TOP 10 TYPES OF COFFEE

Viennese coffees

1 Melange
This is a blend of strong coffee and hot milk, served with foamed milk or whipped cream on the top.

2 Grosser Brauner
A large cup of black coffee, steamed like an espresso, and served with a tiny jug of cream on the side.

3 Kleiner Brauner
This is the smaller version of the *Grosser Brauner* and is also served with cream.

4 Grosser Schwarzer
The drink for real coffee addicts – a large, strong cup of black coffee – like a double espresso.

5 Kleiner Schwarzer
As the smaller version of the *Grosser Schwarzer*, this is simply a small cup of black coffee, similar to an espresso.

6 Verlängerter
This is the "lengthened" variety of a *Brauner*, a coffee weakened slightly with hot water and served with milk instead of cream.

7 Kaisermelange
Not to everyone's taste, a *Kaisermelange* is a strong black coffee mixed with egg yolk, honey and Cognac.

8 Einspänner
In this famous drink, strong black coffee is served in a glass with a crown of whipped cream on top.

9 Fiaker
A large cup of coffee is refined with rum and whipped cream. It is named after the city's horse-drawn carriages.

10 Eiskaffee
For this drink, cold coffee is served with vanilla ice cream and whipped cream in a tall glass.

🔟 Restaurants

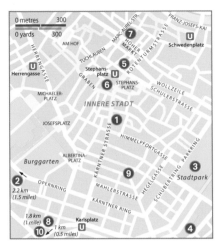

② Die Wäscherei

This restaurant (see p111) is a great spot for brunch. Vienna's young residents flock here for its superb €17.50 all-you-can-eat menu. Set in an old laundry, Die Wäscherei serves vegetarian, Middle Eastern, Mediterranean and Asian fare, alongside Viennese comfort food.

③ Steirereck

With its fabulous service, culinary artistry and excellent Stadtpark location, the two-Michelin-starred Steirereck is counted among the best restaurants (see p99) in the city. Chef Heinz Reitbauer's menus exhibit stunning flair and have both regional and international influences. The specialities here include sturgeon fillets with day lily, aubergine and watercress, and the freshwater mountain fish, char, which is cooked at the table in hot beeswax. Its cellar holds around 25,000 bottles of international and Austrian wines. It's best to book ahead.

① Restaurant im Hotel Ambassador

Located on the first floor of the Hotel Ambassador, this gourmet restaurant (see p99) offers traditional Austrian and international cuisine with contemporary touches. Seasonal dishes, such as venison and wild boar, feature on the menu, as well as fish and vegetarian fare. The modern dining room is pleasantly light and spacious. Reservations are essential.

Modern interior of Steirereck, one of the best restaurants in Vienna

Inside the elegant EssDur

4 EssDur

A marriage of music and food, the award-winning EssDur is the in-house restaurant (see p125) of the Konzerthaus (see p73). It specializes in cutting-edge contemporary Austrian cuisine, which is served in a bright modern dining room.

5 Wrenkh

This vegan and vegetarian spot (see p99) is one of the city's most popular restaurants for non-meat eaters. The renowned Wrenkh brothers preside over the menu, which focuses on seasonal and local ingredients. The siblings also run an acclaimed vegetarian cooking school onsite.

6 DO & CO Stephansplatz

Sumptuous dishes are served in an elegant setting at this modern bistro (see p99) on the top floor of Haas House. Enjoy spectacular rooftop views against the backdrop of the St Stephen's Cathedral as you dine on an eclectic range of Austrian classics teamed with Asian delicacies.

7 Silvio Nickol

Housed in the 19th-century Palais Cobur, this stylish, two-Michelin-starred restaurant (see p99) serves eye-catching haute cuisine. Dishes here include duck with blood sausage and catfish with capers and raisins. There's an excellent selection of wines, too, including some rare vintages.

8 Steman

This restaurant is the epitome of old-fashioned and inexpensive traditional cooking (see p119). A rustic Viennese tavern with bright green fridges and a wood-furnished dining room with white tablecloths and parquet floors, it may be overlooked by gourmet magazines, but is always packed with punters to the high white ceilings every weekday. The *Wiener schnitzel* and goulash are to die for. Reservations are a must.

9 Zum Schwarzen Kameel

A very popular spot with the locals, this old-world restaurant and bar (see p99) offers hearty Viennese cuisine, with dishes such as turkey skewers, spare ribs or cod served with tartar sauce. The bar also serves up a wide variety of sandwiches and snacks. During the summer months, diners can eat alfresco in the shaded outdoor seating area.

Diners at Zum Schwarzen Kameel

10 Zu den drei Buchteln

Neither the decor nor the cuisine has changed since 1950 in this temple (see p119) to Bohemian classic dishes. Specialities include the eponymous *buchteln* yeast cakes. Meticulously prepared by two charming Czech ladies, the food is traditional and portions ample. This is the ideal place to visit if you want to get a taste of classic Viennese flavours.

🔟 Heurigen

Pretty Fuhrgassl-Huber *heuriger*

1 Fuhrgassl-Huber
Neustift am Walde 68 ■ Bus 35A ■ 01 440 14 05 ■ €€

With seating for 800 people, this busy *heurigen* (wine tavern), located on the edge of the Vienna Woods *(see p128)*, is one of the city's largest wine taverns. Glasses of the most recent vintage can be accompanied with food from the buffet, which serves everything from smoked ham to delicious *Wiener schnitzel (see p74)*.

2 Hengl-Haselbrunner
Iglaseegasse 10 ■ U-Bahn U4; bus 10A, 39A; tram 37, 38, 54S ■ 01 320 33 30 ■ €€

Grinzing *(see p128)* was once a small community of wine-growers, but now it has one of the highest densities of *heurigen* in Vienna. Slightly off the beaten track, Hengl-Haselbrunner offers excellent red and white wines, plus a buffet of regional specialities.

3 Wieninger
Stammersdorfer Strasse 31 ■ Bus 30A; tram 30, 31 ■ 01 290 10 12 ■ Closed Nov–mid-Apr ■ No credit cards ■ €€

This family business serves excellent wines that perfectly complement great food. Largely frequented by locals, Wieninger is less expensive than *heurigen* located in the more famous communities of Grinzing and Nussdorf.

4 Kierlinger
Kahlenberger Strasse 20 ■ Train Nussdorf; tram D ■ 01 370 22 64 ■ No credit cards ■ €

The white wines of this traditional tavern are counted among Vienna's best – be sure to sample a glass of their Chardonnay or Weissburgunder. Kierlinger is also known for its tasty Liptauer spread, made of cheese with paprika, onions, gherkins and spices. The *heuriger* has a large garden, and cultural events take place in the evening all year round.

5 Mayer am Pfarrplatz
Pfarrplatz 2 ■ U-Bahn U4; bus 38A; tram D ■ 01 370 12 87 ■ €€

The historic building now occupied by Mayer am Pfarrplatz was once the home of Ludwig van Beethoven *(see p60)*. He spent the summer of 1817 here when he hoped to find relief for his worsening deafness. Today, you can soak up the atmosphere and dine on excellent food and home-produced wines. It's an acclaimed winery and has won many national and international prizes. Traditional Viennese live music is played every Friday at 7pm.

6 Sirbu
Kahlenberger Strasse 210 ■ Train and taxi Nussdorf, bus 38A ■ 01 320 59 28 ■ Closed Sun & Nov–Mar ■ €

Perched on Kahlenberg mountain *(see p129)*, this *heuriger* is set amid luscious vineyards, and is lovely at night. The usual *heurigen* dishes and home-grown wines are served.

Visitors enjoying the scenery at Sirbu

7 Zahel

Maurer Hauptplatz 9 ■ Tram 60
■ **01 889 13 18 (call for openings)**
■ **Closed Sun** ■ **No credit cards** ■ €

The flavourful and aromatic reds and whites from Zahel, a charming winery, should not be missed. This *heuriger's* buffet has a varying selection of à la carte dishes.

Outdoor seating at Zimmermann

8 Zimmermann

Mitterwurzergasse 20 ■ Bus 35A, 39A ■ **01 440 12 07** ■ **Closed Mon & Nov–mid-Mar** ■ €

In rural isolation on the edge of the Vienna Woods, Zimmermann has a zoo with all sorts of small animals, and there is a great friendly, family atmosphere. Enjoy a glass of the new vintages with dishes from the buffet and, in summer, sit out amid the pretty Neustift vineyards.

9 Weingut Heuriger Muth

Probusgasse 10 ■ Tram 37, bus 38A
■ **01 318 55 95** ■ €€

This *heurigen* is one of Vienna's oldest wine taverns. It has a large and shady outdoor seating area that is perfect for the summer months. It often hosts live music performances.

10 Christ

Amtsstrasse 14 ■ S-Bahn 4
■ **01 292 51 52** ■ **Closed even months** ■ €

The Christ family has been producing wine for 400 years, winning many awards. Traditional and cosy with a peaceful garden, this *heurigen* serves seasonal traditional food, such as asparagus, mushroom or game.

TOP 10 DRINKS

1 White Wines
Austria's superb sweet dessert wines are among the world's best. Vienna is the only capital in the world that produces wine. The main varieties are Grüner Veltliner and Weissburgunder.

2 Red Wines
Austria also produces excellent red wines, including Zweigelt, Blauer Portugieser and Blaufränkisch.

3 Gespritzter
Sparkling water mixed with table wine is an all-time favourite in Austria, particularly in summer.

4 Sparkling Wines
The Austrian sparkling wine Sekt is an increasingly popular drink.

5 Beers
Several breweries in Vienna produce very good, malty beers. Restaurants and bars usually offer a *Seidl* (0.33 litre/ 0.7 pt) or a *Krügel* (0.5 litre/1pt).

6 Soft Drinks
Apple juice and grape juice mixed (*gespritzt*) with sparkling water is a popular soft drink in Vienna, as is *Almdudler*, a herbal lemonade.

7 Sturm
For a few short weeks during the autumn, fermenting grape juice is available. Although it tastes sweet, it is alcoholic and quite powerful.

8 Mulled Wines
Around Christmas, hot spicy wine and punch are warming and very popular.

9 Coffee
Vienna's first coffee house opened in 1683; the city's coffee house culture was awarded UNESCO status in 2011.

10 Schnapps
A distilled eau de vie made from fruits such as apricots or juniper berries.

Bottles of schnapps

For a key to restaurant price ranges see p99

🔟 Markets, Malls and Department Stores

Luxury goods on display in the Steffl department store

1 Steffl
MAP N4 ■ Kärntner Strasse 19

This major department store is located in the heart of the city. You will find mainly designer names such as Ralph Lauren and Calvin Klein on its five floors, but there are also perfumes, cosmetic products and home decor items on sale. The top floor affords great views over the rooftops and the Sky Bar (see p97) offers excellent cocktails.

2 Naschmarkt
Unmissable for any visitor interested in busy, colourful markets, the Naschmarkt (see p116) has everything from fruit and vegetables to a Saturday flea market.

3 Karmelitermarkt
MAP C5 ■ Im Werd, Krummbaumgasse, Leopoldsgasse & Haidgasse

Monday through Saturday, a market takes place on the square encircled by these four streets. It's a bustling spot where you can purchase vegetables, fruit, meat and Turkish food, and check out kosher butchers as well as grocery shops. On weekends, several farmers and vendors set up their tables and sell their produce.

4 Ringstrassen Galerien
MAP N6 ■ Kärntner Ring 5–7 & 9–13

This elegant shopping centre is Vienna's most expensive retail area, with designer clothes as well as jewellery and gourmet food. The shops are interspersed with cafés and restaurants.

5 Wien Mitte The Mall
MAP R4 ■ Landstrasser Hauptstrasse 1b

This spacious, modern shopping mall is located at Wien Mitte station. You'll find all kinds of goods here, from fashion labels to shoe shops, electronic items to

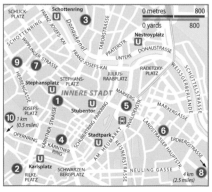

jewellery, as well as a supermarket that is open on Sundays. There are cafés and restaurants aplenty for weary shoppers.

6 Rochusmarkt
MAP R4 ■ Landstrasser Hauptstrasse 51

Just outside the Rochusgasse metro station, this small market has some 30 permanent stalls offering mainly fruit, vegetables, flowers and fresh meat. On Saturdays it doubles in size, when farmers from further afield come to sell their home-grown crops.

7 Am Hof
MAP M2

The Baroque Am Hof square, with its unique architectural surroundings and cobbled streets, is the perfect setting for an antiques market. Vendors offer all kinds of antique goods on Fridays and Saturdays, but the market is best known for its second-hand books – you might be lucky and find a rare or early edition of your favourite title.

8 Gasometer

These four striking, round industrial buildings *(see p66)* were constructed between 1896 and 1899 to store gas. They were converted in 2001 by four renowned architects (Coop Himmelblau, Jean Nouvel, Manfred Wehdorn and Wilhelm Holzbauer) into an events hall, 615 apartments, a students' hall of residence and a shopping centre with around 70 shops offering everything from fashion to electronic goods. The four separate buildings are connected by glazed corridors.

Browsing Freyung's Easter market

9 Freyung
MAP L2

In medieval times both festivals and executions took place on the Freyung, but it is largely markets that are held here today. It's a real Viennese experience. A farmers' market selling mainly organic produce takes place every two weeks and, just before Christmas, a bustling festive market sells all sorts of handmade art and vendors offer alcoholic punch. It also has a picturesque Easter market.

10 Gerngross
MAP F2 ■ Mariahilfer Strasse 47–48

One of Vienna's largest department stores, Gerngross has goods ranging from designer clothing to middle-of-the-range labels, from trendy fashion accessories to home decor. There is a sushi restaurant and a café on the top floor, both offering an excellent view over the bustling shopping street *(see p117)* down below.

The iconic Gasometer buildings

TOP 10 Vienna for Free

Schloss Schönbrunn gardens

1 Schloss Schönbrunn Gardens

Although entry to Vienna's grandest palace is pricey, visitors can stroll the delightful gardens for free. Schloss Schönbrunn *(see pp42–5)* is a horticultural wonder, with sumptuous planting and pretty fountains.

2 Magical Music

Summer nights concert: www. sommernachtskonzert.at ▪ Donauinselfest: www.donauinselfest.at ▪ Fest der Freude: www.festderfreude.at

In June, free open-air concerts include the Vienna Philharmonic in Schloss Schönbrunn gardens and three days of live music at Europe's biggest free party at Donauinsel. Meanwhile, the Fest der Freude sees the Wiener Symphoniker orchestra perform on Heldenplatz.

Open-air Vienna Philharmonic concert

3 The Hofburg

While many of the dazzling imperial residences of the Hofburg palace *(see pp16–19)* charge for entry, the maze of stone passages, Michaelerkirche and Augustinerkirche can be visited for free.

4 Tours of the Rathaus

Free state room tours of Vienna's Rathaus *(see p108)* reveal some of the city's lesser-known political secrets and are rich in controversy, power struggles and mayoral intrigue.

5 Walking Tour

WomWalk: departs Wombat's, Rechte Wienzeile 35, Naschmarkt; 01 897 23 36; 10:30am Mon, Wed, Fri & Sat; www.wombats-hostels.com

Take advantage of the city's only free walking tour, departing four days a week from the Wombats Hostel in Naschmarkt. It's a great way for solo travellers to make new friends.

6 Danube Dipping

The beach at the tip of the summer party island of Donauinsel in the middle of the Danube river is a designated FKK zone for clothes-optional sun-bathing. FKK stands for *freikörperkultur*, meaning "culture of free bodies". Stripping off in this verdant waterfront setting costs nothing and you can also drink at the bars here *au naturel*.

7 Sankt-Marxer-Friedhof

Take a leisurely stroll around the famous St Marx Cemetery (see p130). Among the medieval tombs, burial chambers and carved crosses, you'll spot a gravestone that honours beloved composer Mozart (his body is thought to be buried elsewhere in a pauper's grave).

8 Museum Entry

Wien Museum: www.wien museum.at

The Kunsthistorisches Museum (see pp22–5), the Belvedere (see pp28–31), the Naturhistorisches Museum (see p107) and several others in Vienna offer free entry to under 19s. Most museums are free on National Day (26 October) and there is also free admission on the first Sunday of the month at all Wien Museum sites.

Prater park and its Ferris wheel

9 Prater

It doesn't cost a penny to wander around the Prater, the large public park (see p64) located in the east of the city. So, unless you want to ride the funfair or dine out at the food stalls, all the magic, music and mayhem of 200 attractions are free.

10 Cinematic Splendour

Rathausplatz ■ Herbert-von-Karajan Platz: www.wien.info

Vienna runs atmospheric open-air cinema screenings of opera, ballet and classical music from July to August. There's also a giant screen on Herbert-von-Karajan Platz, which shows Staatsoper (see pp36–7) opera and ballet concerts all summer.

TOP 10 BUDGET TIPS

A WienMobil Bike docking station

1 Make use of the free hour's bike hire from WienMobil Bike (www.wienerlini en.at), Vienna's public rental scheme (see p137). Pick up a bike from one of the docking stations and return it to another station within an hour.

2 For a cheaper alternative to an open-top bus ride take the tram: a scenic option at a fraction of the price (www.wienerlinien.at).

3 Pick up a money-saving Vienna PASS (www.viennapass.com) for free entry to over 60 top attractions, museums and monuments plus discount travel.

4 Maximize cheap travel by avoiding peak travel times and buying a multi-day travel pass for 24, 48 or 72 hours (www.wienerlinien.at).

5 To take a self-guided walking tour, download a free map from City Walks (www.city-walks.info/Vienna). A stroll along the Danube Canal, Vienna's open-air gallery, lets you admire the quirky graffiti adorning its banks.

6 Make your way to Neubau (see p108) for the city's best cheap eats. Some places charge only what you can afford to pay.

7 Don't waste your money on fancy bottled waters as Vienna's high-quality drinking water comes straight from a sparkling mountain springs.

8 No need to rack up hefty mobile bills while you're exploring Vienna as free Wi-Fi hotspots are available in almost all central public places.

9 Last-minute cut-priced theatre and music tickets are available from venues on the day (www.viennaconcerts.com).

10 Visit the Saturday flea market (flohmarkt) in the Naschmarkt (see p116) for unique shoestring bargains.

🔟 Festivals

into a bustling hub for music lovers. Every evening crowds flock to watch pop concerts, musicals, ballet opera and operetta performances broadcast on a huge screen. Just as popular are the many food stalls where Mexican, Japanese, Greek as well as Austrian specialities can all be found.

Colourful painted Easter eggs

1 Easter Markets
Mar/Apr

Austria's Easter tradition is to decorate branches of pussy willow with painted eggshells hung on string. Easter Egg Markets are also held on squares and in front of churches.

2 Wiener Festwochen
May/Jun

This annual festival held at venues including the MuseumsQuartier (see pp34–5), the Ronacher and Theater an der Wien (see p72) includes theatre and dance productions.

3 Jazzfest
Mid-Jun–early Jul

Traditional homes of classical music such as the State Opera and the Konzerthaus (see p73) turn into jazz venues during the annual Jazzfest, where you can see world-famous jazz musicians perform all over the city.

4 Oper Klosterneuburg
Jul

This festival stages glamorous performances of opera classics in the courtyard of Klosterneuburg abbey (see p130), the palatial religious foundation that dominates the town of the same name just north of Vienna. There are also fascinating behind-the-scenes workshops for children.

5 MusikFilmFestival
Jul–Aug

Every year the square in front of Vienna's Town Hall (see p108) turns

6 ImPulsTanz
Jul–Aug

Vienna turns into the capital of dance when the international dance festival takes place at venues such as the Burg and Akademietheater.

Dancer performing at ImPulsTanz

7 Viennale
Oct

Vienna's international film festival, the Viennale, features pre-release and independent films from around the world. Screenings take place at the Gartenbau, Urania and Metro cinemas, among other venues.

8 Wien Modern
Late Oct–Nov

Founded by Claudio Abbado in 1988, Wien Modern is one of few genuinely successful festivals for post-1945 and contemporary "classical" music in Europe. The emphasis is on the avant-garde, and the concerts play to large and enthusiastic audiences.

One of Vienna's Christmas markets

9 Christmas Markets
Nov–Dec

In the weeks leading up to Christmas you'll find numerous festive markets across Vienna's squares and pedestrianized zones. The stalls sell small gifts and Christmas decorations, as well as punch and hot spiced wine to warm you on cold winter evenings.

10 Ball Season
Dec–Feb

Viennese life revolves around the waltz, at least between Christmas and Lent, when the calendar is full with evenings of dancing. Balls in the Hofburg palace are the most splendid, but there are dances every evening in many of Vienna's hotels, concert halls and, once a year, in the Staatsoper (see pp36–7).

Guests at the Staatsoper ball

TOP 10 RELIGIOUS FESTIVALS

Christmas mass in Stephansdom

1 Epiphany
6 Jan
Children dress as the Three Wise Men and bring news of Christ's birth.

2 Easter
Mar/Apr
The resurrection of Christ is celebrated with fires and light processions.

3 Christ's Ascension
May/Jun (40 days after Easter)
Celebrated to mark the day that Christ ascended to heaven.

4 Pentecost
May/Jun (50 days after Easter)
Celebrates the Holy Ghost being sent to unite the world's peoples.

5 Corpus Christi
May/Jun (60 days after Easter)
Processions are held and a monstrance is carried from altar to altar.

6 Mary's Ascension
15 Aug
This day commemorates the Virgin Mary's ascension to heaven.

7 All Saints' Day
1 Nov
Austrians visit the graves of their loved ones to light candles and lay wreaths.

8 Feast of the Immaculate Conception
8 Dec
On this day, St Anne conceived a daughter, the Virgin Mary.

9 Christmas Eve
24 Dec
The most important day of the festive celebrations, as families gather around the Christmas tree and open presents.

10 Christmas Day
25 Dec
A holy day when people attend church and visit their families.

Vienna
Area by Area

Bird's-eye view of Vienna from the
North Tower of Stephansdom

🔟 Central Vienna

With cobbled streets, narrow alleys, quiet squares and a wealth of historic buildings, Vienna's atmospheric heart is brimming with famous landmarks and reminders of both Roman and Habsburg rule, yet it also hosts the *crème de la crème* of shops, restaurants and the city's famous cafés and coffee shops. Several of these are located on the three spacious pedestrian zones of Kärntner Strasse, Graben and Kohlmarkt. These streets form an ideal stage for outdoor performers and make for a pleasant stroll from the State Opera to the Hofburg.

Art Nouveau Anker Uhr clock by Franz von Matsch

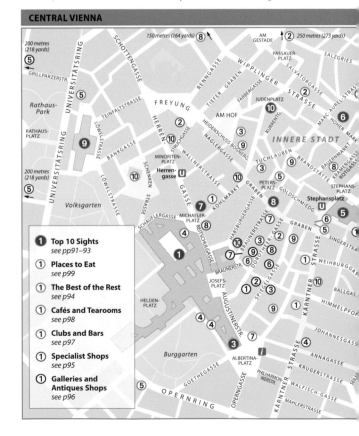

CENTRAL VIENNA

1. **Top 10 Sights**
   see pp91–93
1. **Places to Eat**
   see p99
1. **The Best of the Rest**
   see p94
1. **Cafés and Tearooms**
   see p98
1. **Clubs and Bars**
   see p97
1. **Specialist Shops**
   see p95
1. **Galleries and Antiques Shops**
   see p96

Impressive façade of the Hofburg palace in Central Vienna

1 The Hofburg

The former imperial palace *(see pp16–21)* may have relinquished its regal position after Austria became a republic in 1918, but the elegance of days gone by is still tangible.

2 Postsparkasse

MAP Q3 ▪ Georg-Coch-Platz 2
▪ Open 10am–5pm Mon–Fri

In the Postsparkasse building (the post office savings bank), Otto Wagner *(see p122)* implemented his principles of combining functionalism with appealing design. Stone panels fixed to the external walls with metal rivets led to the building being nicknamed "a box of nails".

Dürer's *Hare* (1502) at the Albertina

3 Albertina

MAP M5 ▪ Albertinaplatz 1
▪ U-Bahn Karlsplatz, Stephansplatz
▪ Open 10am–6pm daily (until 9pm Wed & Fri) ▪ Adm (under 19s free)
▪ www.albertina.at

The Hall of Muses and Rococo Room are two of the most magnificent of the 20 Habsburg State Rooms in the Albertina palace. The palace houses temporary exhibitions in addition to seven major art collections, ranging from contemporary art to graphic, architectural and photographic art, plus period fabrics and costumes.

4 Ruprechtskirche
MAP N2 ■ Ruprechtsplatz
■ **Open 10am–noon & 3–5pm Mon–Fri**

This modest church holds the title of Vienna's oldest place of worship, built in the 9th century after the fall of Vindobona (see p48) as part of the settlements within the Roman city walls. The stone edifice was the city's main church until the end of the 12th century, when Stephansdom became the most important centre of worship in town. Both east windows date back to the 13th century and have survived the ages untouched as Vienna's oldest works of stained glass.

Stunning exterior of Stephansdom

5 Stephansdom
At the geographical epicentre of the city, the spectacular Gothic St Stephen's Cathedral (see pp12–15) dominates the skyline with its imposing towers and its 137-m- (450-ft-) high spire.

6 Anker Uhr
MAP N2 ■ Hoher Markt 10/11

The Anker Uhr clock spans two wings of an insurance company building and was installed between 1911 and 1917 by Franz von Matsch. Every day, 12 pairs of ornate figures, each symbolizing a period in Vienna's history, step forward on the hour. At noon, all figures parade across the bridge to the tune of classical music.

JEWISH VIENNA

Until 1938, most of Vienna's thriving Jewish community lived in Leopoldstadt, an area famous for its theatres, cabarets and synagogues. However, the rise of anti-Semitism under the Nazis lead to the decline of the Jewish Quarter; during this time almost 150,000 Jews fled the country, with another 65,000 murdered under the Nazi regime. Although many Jews have now moved to the nearby Karmeliter quarter, this area still retains its Jewish heritage, with the stunning "city temple" synagogue, vibrant Karmelitermarkt and many kosher restaurants and shops.

7 Looshaus
MAP L3 ■ Michaelerplatz 3
■ **Open 8am–3pm Mon–Wed & Fri, 8am–5:30pm Thu**

No other building triggered so much controversy in Vienna as the Looshaus, completed in 1911. Emperor Franz Joseph thought the functional building ruined the square's look and had the curtains closed at his Hofburg palace to avoid looking at it. Four floors are covered in green marble but the building's plain upper floors caused uproar. Today it is home to a bank.

8 Pestsäule
MAP M3 ■ Graben

The extravagant Baroque Pestsäule (Plague Column) was erected by Habsburg emperor Leopold I in the year 1679 to commemorate Vienna's deliverance from the horrific plague epidemic that killed more than 100,000 people. Standing on Graben, one of the city's finest shopping boulevards, this 18-m- (70-ft-) tall monument is dedicated to the Holy Trinity. The lavish confection depicts a set of gold-embellished angels and cherubs, symbols of the Trinity, and even the Emperor himself.

The gilded Pestsäule

⑨ Burgtheater
MAP K2 ▪ Universitätsring 2 ▪ Guided tours 3pm daily; call 01 514 44 41 40 ▪ Adm

The Burg *(see p71)*, as it's called affectionately by the Viennese, was among the first theatres to be built in the German-speaking world. Architects Gottfried Semper and Carl von Hasenauer designed this spectacular building with its Renaissance façade over a period of 14 years (1874–88). On its completion, the Court Theatre, founded in 1776, moved into the new building on the Ringstrasse. A grand staircase with frescoes by Gustav Klimt and his brother Ernst leads from the foyer to the auditorium.

The Burgtheater's splendid staircase

⑩ Misrachi-Haus
MAP M2 ▪ Judenplatz 8 ▪ Open 10am–6pm Sun–Thu, 10am–2pm Fri ▪ Adm (under 18s free) ▪ www.jmw.at

In 2000, during the construction of a Holocaust memorial by British artist Rachel Whiteread on Judenplatz, the archaeological remains of a medieval synagogue were discovered on site. The excavation site is now open to the public and a museum is devoted to the life, work and religion of the city's medieval Jewish community. You can also take a virtual walk around the 15th-century Jewish quarter.

A DAY'S STROLL IN CENTRAL VIENNA

▶ MORNING

Begin the day at the magnificent **Stephansdom** *(see pp12–15)*. Catch the morning sun beaming through the medieval features, and stroll around the cathedral's Gothic features. It is well worth climbing the South Tower or taking the lift up the North Tower for stunning views over the rooftops. For a mid-morning break, head to the far end of the square and enjoy a cup of tea in **Haas & Haas** *(see p95)*.

Wander the web of narrow streets around the cathedral but arrive at Hoher Markt at noon to watch the historic Viennese figures of the **Anker Uhr** march by.

There are many places to have lunch, but on a sunny day pick **DO & CO Stephansplatz** *(see p99)* overlooking the cathedral.

AFTERNOON

Spend the early afternoon in Graben and Kohlmarkt, exploring antiques shops and galleries, until you reach the **Hofburg** palace *(see pp16–21)*. With its various collections, select those that interest you most, but don't miss the state apartments where Emperor Franz Joseph lived.

Exit the palace through the huge Michaeler Gate, then pass the **Looshaus**, before treating yourself to a piece of Sachertorte and a coffee at **Café Demel** *(see p98)*.

Finally, if you're visiting in winter, take tram 1 going clockwise from Karlsplatz to Schwedenplatz to see the floodlit buildings by night.

See map on pp90–91 ←

The Best of the Rest

1 Franziskanerplatz
MAP N4 ■ Franziskanerplatz

This charming square is home to the Franziskanerkirche *(see p51)*, pretty houses and the Moses fountain (1798).

2 Altes Rathaus
MAP N2 ■ Wipplingerstrasse 8
■ Closed to the public

The Habsburgs confiscated this palace in 1316 from Otto von Haymo, who had conspired against them. It functioned as the town hall until 1883.

3 Kirche am Hof
MAP M2 ■ Am Hof 7

Emperor Ferdinand III's widow had this monumental church built in 1662. It is more reminiscent of a palace than a place of worship.

4 Heiligenkreuzerhof
MAP P3 ■ Heiligenkreuzerhof

A tranquil courtyard featuring a set of 17th- and 18th-century apartment buildings and a medieval chapel.

5 Peterskirche
MAP M3 ■ Petersplatz

This Baroque church has a dramatic and ornate high altar and frescoes by Johann Michael Rottmayr.

Akademie der Wissenschaften interior

6 Akademie der Wissenschaften
MAP P3 ■ Dr-Ignaz-Seipel-Platz 2

This ornate Rococo building (1755) was formerly the site of Vienna University. The Academy of Sciences hall staged the premiere of Joseph Haydn's *The Creation* in 1808.

7 Memorial against War and Fascism

Artist Alfred Hrdlicka's powerful sculpture *(see p54)* memorializes World War II and the atrocities of Nazi governance that led to the death of nearly 65,000 Viennese Jews in concentration camps.

8 Börse
MAP L1 ■ Schottenring 16

Once the home of the Vienna Stock Exchange, this Theophil von Hansen Classicist building, built 1874–7, is now used by the government.

9 Kapuzinerkirche
MAP M4 ■ Neuer Markt

Built in 1618, the simple design of this church is in line with the Capuchin order's doctrine. Emperor Matthias (1557–1619) established a crypt *(see p63)* for the Habsburgs here.

10 Minoritenkirche
MAP L3 ■ Minoritenplatz 2

When Duke Leopold VI returned safely from a crusade in 1219, he built a church on this site. Its medieval character is still visible.

Façade of the Baroque Peterskirche

See map on pp90–91

Specialist Shops

1 Haas & Haas
MAP N3 ▪ Stephansplatz 4

Just behind Stephansdom, this shop offers more than 200 assorted fruit teas, black teas, herbal teas and many tea accessories. The marzipan sweets and chocolates are divine.

2 Xocolat
MAP L2 ▪ Freyung 2, in the Palais Ferstel

Everything in this little shop revolves around chocolate, with more than 120 varieties from all over the world, as well as books on the subject.

The tempting interior of Xocolat

3 Doblinger
MAP M4 ▪ Dorotheergasse 10

This music publishing house, which has been in business for 125 years, has every music score a musician can dream of. Be it classical or contemporary music, Doblinger has it.

4 Mayr & Fessler
MAP N4 ▪ Kärntner Strasse 37

This is the best address for top-of-the-range fountain pens, as well as diaries and organizers. It has a wide range of Italian writing and wrapping paper as well as notebooks and accessories.

5 Gmundner Ceramics
MAP D2 ▪ Stadiongasse 7

Pretty Austrian hand-painted pottery is produced at Gmunden in Upper Austria. The traditional decoration of green-on-white looks sloshed-on, but perfect. This shop offers a wide range of wares and patterns just outside the Ring behind Parliament.

6 Shakespeare & Co
MAP N2 ▪ Sterngasse 2

This tiny bookshop is brimming with character and is the best place to go for contemporary English literature. There are also very good travel and poetry sections.

7 Knize
MAP M3 ▪ Graben 13

Custom-made clothing has been the focus of this elegant establishment for nearly 150 years. The shop itself is internationally admired, as Adolf Loos turned it into a masterpiece in 1910.

8 Loden Plankl
MAP L3 ▪ Michaelerplatz 6

This old family business offers traditional Austrian clothing ranging from Loden coats and jackets to beautiful Dirndl dresses and Lederhosen (leather trousers). It also stocks modern variations of traditional garments.

9 Augarten Flagship Store
MAP M4 ▪ Spiegelgasse 3

The porcelain at the city outlet of Vienna's historic factory ranges from fine tableware to Wiener Werkstätte designs and modern objets d'art.

10 Meinl am Graben
MAP M3 ▪ Am Graben 19

One of Vienna's best delicatessens, the upscale Meinl am Graben has a great selection of chocolates, dessert wines, coffee and fresh produce.

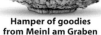

Hamper of goodies from Meinl am Graben

Galleries and Antiques Shops

Inside the Dorotheum Auction House

1 Dorotheum Auction House
MAP M4 ■ Dorotheergasse 17
■ www.dorotheum.at

Vienna is well known for its antiques, and Dorotheergasse is one of the main areas to head for if this is your interest. At the city's main auction house, in operation since 1907, you can buy everything from antique furniture to jewellery and paintings.

2 Alte Kunst und Militaria
MAP M4 ■ Plankengasse 7
■ www.militaria-koeck.at

Books, guns, sabers, medals and old uniforms from past military campaigns are stocked here.

3 Wissenschaftliches Kabinett
MAP M4 ■ Spiegelgasse 23
■ www.wisskab.com

This is a fascinating place to browse unique objects such as antique surgical saws, phrenology skulls and chess pieces.

4 Galerie Ambiente
MAP N3 ■ Lugeck 1 ■ www.ambientegalerieambiente.at

Beautiful and innovative furniture, from Viennese designers and manufacturers such as Josef Hoffmann and Thonet, is sold at Ambiente. They can also arrange shipping to get your goods sent directly home.

5 Antiquariat Inlibris
MAP J3 ■ Rathausstrasse 19
■ www.inlibris.at

Scientific books, early prints and Austrian memorabilia are just some of the specialities at this antiquarian bookshop, established in 1883.

6 Wiener Interieur
MAP M4 ■ Dorotheergasse 14
■ www.wiener-interieur.at

Situated among Dorotheergasse's many galleries and antiques shops, Wiener Interieur has beautiful jewellery from the beginning of the 20th century up to the 1960s. This is a gem-lover's paradise.

7 Galerie Hofstätter
MAP M4 ■ Bräunerstrasse 7
■ www.galerie-hofstaetter.com

This gallery organizes several major exhibitions a year of Austrian post-war and contemporary artists.

8 Galerie Hilger
MAP M4 ■ Dorotheergasse 5
■ www.hilger.at

Early 20th-century art and a variety of contemporary Austrian and international artists are shown in nine exhibitions a year.

9 Galerie Charim
MAP M4 ■ Dorotheergasse 12
■ www.charimgalerie.at

This gallery in the former Palais Gatterburg specializes in Austrian art, including object art and new media, as well as photography.

10 Sonja Reisch
MAP M3 ■ Bräunerstrasse 10
■ www.antiquitaeten-reisch.com

Silver- and tableware, as well as jewellery, glass and decorative objects from the Biedermeier era, are sold at this shop.

See map on pp90–91

Clubs and Bars

1 American Bar
MAP N4 ▪ Kärntner Passage
▪ www.loosbar.at

In a simple yet sophisticated Adolf Loos building, this bar is one of the most beautiful nightspots in town. It also serves delicious cocktails.

2 Planter's Club
MAP C4 ▪ Zelinkagasse 4
▪ www.plantersclub.com

This historical bar, with its teak wood panelling, evokes a tea plantation house. You can choose from more than 300 whiskies, 90 rums and many mouthwatering cocktails.

3 Bermuda Bräu
MAP P2 ▪ Rabensteig 6
▪ www.bermuda-braeu.at

In a party area called the Bermuda Triangle, this lively pub offers superb draught beer served in clay jugs, as well as a variety of bottled beers. It has a dance floor in the basement.

4 Palmenhaus
This renovated imperial greenhouse hosts a stylish restaurant (see p99) and bar with fine Austrian wines and occasional live DJ nights.

5 Volksgarten
MAP K4 ▪ Burgring 1 ▪ www. volksgarten.at

The Volksgarten is one of the city's most established party zones, with a varied mix of music. The fabulous garden is an ideal setting in summer.

6 Onyx Bar
MAP N3 ▪ Haas-Haus, Stephansplatz 12, 7th floor ▪ www. docohotel.com

Vienna's in-crowd gathers in this bar with its fine view of Stephansdom (see pp12–15). Snacks, cocktails and groovy background music are on offer.

7 Meinz
MAP N2 ▪ Seitenstettengasse 5
▪ www.meinz.wien

Soak up some live jazz, blues, soul and modern music while sipping on creative cocktails at this intimate bar.

8 Jazzland
MAP N2 ▪ Franz-Josefs-Kai 29
▪ www.jazzland.at

Housed in a 500-year-old cellar, this popular and lively venue (see p73) is the oldest jazz club in Austria.

9 Roter Engel
MAP P2 ▪ Rabensteig 5 ▪ www. roterengel.at

Music is the speciality of this bar, with local artists playing rock, pop, funk and soul every Monday to Thursday.

10 Skybar
MAP N4 ▪ Kärntner Strasse 19
▪ www.steffl-vienna.at

Located inside the department store Steffl (see p82), this swanky bar has a great vibe and a view over Vienna's rooftops. The cocktails are excellent.

The stylish Skybar has great city views

Cafés and Tearooms

1 Café Demel
MAP M3 ■ Kohlmarkt 14
■ www.demel.com

An opulent interior and central location makes Demel (see p76) an ideal rest stop for snacks or pastries.

2 Café Hawelka
MAP M3 ■ Dorotheergasse 6
■ www.hawelka.at

Open until 1am on weekends, Café Hawelka (see p77) features old-world decor. Don't ask for a menu – there isn't one – but do try the sweet rolls.

3 Café Diglas
MAP P2 ■ Fleischmarkt 16
■ www.fleischmarkt.diglas.at

A charming, small traditional café, Diglas (see p76) sells mouthwatering cakes and you can even watch some being made in the historic bakery.

4 Café Hofburg
MAP L4 ■ Innerer Burghof 1
■ www.cafe-hofburg.at

Expect sumptuous elegance at this regal address where terrace seating overlooking the Hofburg palace's inner courtyard offers a window on 600 years of Habsburg history.

5 Café Landtmann
MAP K2 ■ Universitätsring 4
■ www.landtmann.at

A temple (see p76) to the traditional concept of a coffee house, with service and prices to match. There's a small terrace for dining al fresco.

6 Café Bräunerhof
MAP M4 ■ Stallburggasse 2
■ 01 512 38 93

Featuring live classical music on Saturdays this place (see p77) is traditional but simple in style, and less expensive than most spots.

7 Café Schwarzenberg
MAP N6 ■ Kärtner Ring 17
■ www.cafe-schwarzenberg.at

Instead of tourists, this distinguished café has long catered to businessmen. It's the oldest café on the Ringstrasse.

8 Café Prückel
MAP Q3 ■ Stubenring 24

A highly popular reworking of the traditional coffee house in 1950s retro design, Prückel (see p77) is close to MAK, the Museum of Applied Arts.

9 Café Korb
MAP M3 ■ Brandstätte 9
■ www.prueckel.at

Tuck into tasty apple strudel at this characterful café. The Art Lounge in its basement organizes art, music, drama and literary events.

10 Café Central
MAP L2 ■ Herrengasse 14
■ www.cafecentral.wien

This café (see p76) modestly claims to be the "true centre" of Vienna, and the lofty vaulted ceilings are said to contain the ego of Sigmund Freud.

Vaulted ceilings of Café Central

Places to Eat

PRICE CATEGORIES
For a three-course meal for one with half
a bottle of wine (or equivalent meal),
taxes and extra charges.
....
€ under €35   **€€** €35–70   **€€€** over €70

① Restaurant im Hotel Ambassador
MAP N4 ■ Kärntnerstrasse 22
■ 01 961 61 620 ■ €€

A menu ranging from traditional
favourites to fish and meat dishes is
served in the sumptuous setting of
one of Vienna's top hotels (see p78).

② Steiereck
MAP Q4 ■ Am Heumarkt 2a,
Stadtpark ■ 01 713 31 68 ■ Closed
Sat & Sun ■ €€€

One of the most highly rated Austrian
restaurants (see p78) makes for an
essential dining experience.

Stylish interior of Fabios

③ Fabios
MAP M3 ■ Tuchlauben 6
■ 01 532 22 22 ■ €€€

Sleek and contemporary, this
Italian restaurant is frequented
by Vienna's glitterati and is one
of the city's trendiest dining spots.

④ Palmenhaus
MAP M5 ■ Burggarten 1
■ 01 533 10 33 ■ €€

This Art Nouveau conservatory
(see p97) offers great views and
good food. There's also dancing
on weekend evenings.

DO & CO Stephansplatz

⑤ DO & CO Stephansplatz
MAP N3 ■ Haas Haus, Stephansplatz 12 ■ 01 535 39 69 ■ €€€

This stylish rooftop venue (see p79)
offers a sophisticated selection of the
best dishes from around the world.

⑥ Silvio Nickol
MAP P4 ■ Palais Coburg,
Coburgbastei 4 ■ 01 518 18 800 ■ €€€

Famous for its tasting menus, the
two-Michelin-starred Silvio Nickol
has an international reputation for
its exquisite contemporary fare.

⑦ Plachutta
MAP N3 ■ Wollzeile 38 ■ 01
512 15 77 ■ €€

This traditional Viennese place is
known for its beef dishes. Don't miss
the tafelspitz with roasted potatoes.

⑧ Wrenkh
MAP N3 ■ Bauernmarkt 10
■ 01 533 15 26 ■ Closed Sun & hols ■ €

One of the most popular vegetarian
restaurants (see p79) in the city.

⑨ Zum Schwarzen Kameel
MAP M3 ■ Bognerstrasse 5
■ 01 533 81 25 ■ €€

This quaint restaurant (see p79)
serves delicious traditional dishes
and international cuisines.

⑩ Stadtbeisl Inigo
MAP P3 ■ Bäckerstrasse 18
■ 01 512 74 51 ■ €

Viennese and international cuisine.
Wine list changes every other month.

See map on pp90–91 ←

🔟 Schottenring and Alsergrund

A large part of this area is inhabited by medical institutions, including the AKH general hospital and the Vienna medical school. This is perhaps not surprising in the area where the psychoanalyst Sigmund Freud lived and worked in the early 20th century. The Votivkirche dominates the skyline and looks across a park towards the city centre.

The famous Art Nouveau Strudlhofstiege staircase in the snow

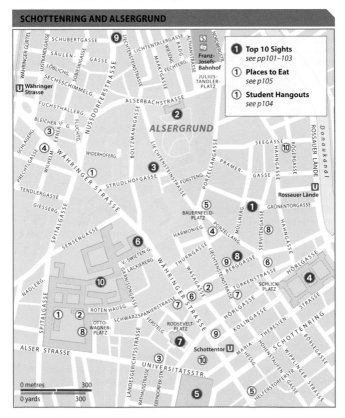

SCHOTTENRING AND ALSERGRUND

1 **Top 10 Sights**
see pp101–103

1 **Places to Eat**
see p105

1 **Student Hangouts**
see p104

Ornate paintings and stucco decorations in the Servitenkirche dome

1 Servitenkirche
MAP B3 ■ Servitengasse 9
■ Open 9am–10pm daily

Although this church is slightly off the beaten track, it is well worth a visit. Built by the Servite convent along with an adjoining monastery in 1651, the interior is decorated with stucco ornaments and frescoes, but the most interesting detail is the 13th-century crucifix to the right of the high altar. Originally the "cross of gallows", it stood at the public execution place on Schlickplatz.

2 Gartenpalais Liechtenstein
MAP A3 ■ Fürstengasse 1
■ Open only for pre-booked tours on Fri (twice a month); call 01 319 57 670 ■ Adm
■ www.palaisliechtenstein.com

Built as the summer residence (see p52) for the Liechtenstein family at the end of the 17th century, the Liechtenstein Garden Palace is Vienna's premier home of Baroque art. The collection includes works by many important artists, such as Raphael, Rubens and Rembrandt. The lovely formal gardens are free and open to the public.

3 Strudlhofstiege
MAP B3 ■ Strudlhofgasse/ Liechtensteinstrasse

This striking Art Nouveau outdoor double staircase, which winds its way down from Strudlhofgasse to Liechtensteinstrasse, was designed by Theodor Jäger in 1910. Two fountains, several lampposts and various ramps create a graceful impression. It became famous in 1951, when Austrian writer Heimito von Doderer published a novel named after the stairway.

4 Rossauer Kaserne
MAP B4 ■ Schlickplatz 6
■ Closed to the public

These huge barracks were created to protect Vienna from attacks from outside the city as well as revolt from within, after the revolutions that took place across Europe in 1848. Together with two other military camps, the Rossauer base formed a strategic triangle. Work on the barracks began in 1864 and was completed six years later. They became the city's police head-quarters after World War II.

**Memorial outside
Rossauer Kaserne**

Vienna University main entrance

5 Vienna University
MAP K1 ■ Universitätsring 1 ■ Open Mon–Sat

The university was founded by Duke Rudolph IV in 1365 and today has around 60,000 students. The present building was constructed in Italian Renaissance style on a former army parade ground following plans by Heinrich Ferstel, and opened in 1884. From the entrance hall with marble columns, grand staircases lead to the lecture theatres and the library. The arcaded courtyard is lined with busts of distinguished professors and the university's eight Nobel Prize winners. The ceremony hall is decorated with frescoes by Gustav Klimt (1895).

6 Josephinum
MAP B3 ■ Währinger Strasse 25 ■ Closed for restoration; check website for details ■ www.josephinum.ac.at

Founded by Emperor Joseph II in 1785, the Josephinum (see p57) was a medical academy where military doctors and general practitioners trained. Today, it houses the Institute for the History of Medicine.

7 Votivkirche
MAP C3 ■ Rooseveltplatz ■ Open 10am–6pm Tue–Sat, 9am–1pm Sun ■ www.votivkirche.at

This striking church (see pp50–51) is part of the Ringstrasse. Inside, there is a museum (closed due to ongoing restoration), with jewelled chalices and other sacred objects. Holy Mass is conducted every second Saturday at 11:15am in multiple languages.

The elaborate exterior of the pretty sandstone Votivkirche

8 Sigmund Freud Museum

MAP B3 ■ Berggasse 19 ■ Open 9am–5pm daily ■ Adm ■ www.freud-museum.at

The founder of psychoanalysis lived in Vienna from 1891 until 1938, when he fled from the National Socialists to London. In his spacious apartment in Berggasse, now a museum, he wrote many famous works and case histories such as *The Interpretation of Dreams*.

Exhibition at Sigmund Freud Museum

9 Schubert's House of Birth

MAP A2 ■ Nussdorfer Strasse 54 ■ Open 10am–1pm & 2–6pm Tue–Sun & public hols ■ Adm (under 19s and every first Sun free)

Franz Schubert *(see p60)* was born in the kitchen of this little first-floor apartment, now a museum, on 31 January 1797 and spent the first four years of his life in the property, known locally as "House of the Red Crab". The museum has information on the composer's life as well as portraits by Schubert's contemporaries.

10 Altes Allgemeines Krankenhaus

MAP B2 ■ Spitalgasse 2

This sprawling former hospital complex with 11 courtyards is a beautiful oasis of calm. In the late 18th century, Emperor Joseph II converted an existing house for the poor into a general hospital, which included a "birth house", a "foundling house", and a "mad house" – today a pathological museum *(see p57)*. The complex is now part of the Vienna University campus.

A DAY IN VIENNA'S STUDENT DISTRICT

▶ MORNING

Start your day at **Vienna University**, exploring the marble entrance hall and the courtyard. Then head towards the beautiful **Votivkirche**, which offers guided tours on the second Saturday of the month at 11am. Walk up Alser Strasse until you reach the **Altes Allgemeines Krankenhaus**, the former general hospital. For a break, choose one of the pubs in the large first courtyard, amid crowds of students.

Head to courtyard 13, where the **Pathologisch-Anatomisches Museum** *(see p57)* is situated. Cut your way to Strudlhofgasse and stride down **Strudlhofstiege** *(see p101)*, where you can already spot the **Gartenpalais Liechtenstein** *(see p101)*. In Porzellangasse you will find several places for lunch.

AFTERNOON

On your way to the **Sigmund Freud Museum**, ensure you pass by **Servitenkirche** *(see p101)* and stop for a glimpse of the Baroque interior. Give yourself enough time browse around Dr Freud's apartment and consulting rooms. For a quick break and a cup of coffee or mint tea, **Florentin 1090** *(see p104)* just across the road is a great spot to rest your feet and gather your thoughts. Later, spend a while people-watching in the **Sigmund Freud Park** *(see p104)*, a popular student hangout in summer.

You can round the day off with a visit to **Votiv Kino** *(Währinger Strasse 12; 01 317 35 71)*, an arts cinema that shows independent films in the original language.

See map on p100 ←

Student Hangouts

1 Stiegl-Ambulanz
MAP C2 ▪ University Campus,
Alser Strasse 4 ▪ www.stiegl-
ambulanz.com
Open all year round, Stiegl-Ambulanz
offers traditional Viennese food at
reasonable prices. It also has a wide
range of beers.

2 Florentin 1090
MAP C3 ▪ Berggasse 8
▪ www.florentin1090.com
A trendy hangout next door to the
LGBTQ+ bookshop Löwenherz, serving
Middle Eastern and Austrian dishes.

3 Cafeteria Maximilian
MAP K1 ▪ Universitätsstrasse 2
▪ 01 405 7149
Right by Vienna University, this
cafeteria serves simple comfort food,
attracting hordes of people, many of
whom stay a while to socialize.

4 Statt-Beisl im WUK
MAP B2 ▪ Währinger
Strasse 59 ▪ www.statt-beisl.info
This former 19th-century locomotive
factory has been cleverly converted
into a cultural centre and operates
a café and restaurant.

5 Juice Factory
MAP C3 ▪ Schottengasse 4
▪ www.juicefactory.at
The natural fruit and vegetable
concoctions at this juice bar help to
refresh and detox. Coffee and smoo-
thie breakfast bowls are also offered.

6 Café Votiv
MAP C3 ▪ Währinger
Strasse 12 ▪ www.votivkino.at
The trendy café within the Votiv
cinema is popular with students
as well as, of course, cinemagoers
before and after film screenings.

7 Charlie P's
MAP C3 ▪ Währinger Strasse 3
▪ www.charlieps.at
A traditional Irish pub, Charlie P's
has a particularly lively atmosphere.
Fish and chips and Guinness are
essential parts of the menu.

8 Gangl
MAP C2 ▪ University Campus,
Alser Strasse 4 ▪ www.gangl.at
Beer on tap, toasted sandwiches
and a cosy atmosphere (as well as
seating outside in summer) attract
a loyal crowd of students here.

9 Café Stein
MAP C3 ▪ Währinger Strasse 6–8
▪ www.cafestein.at
This spot has seating inside and out,
and offers a good view of the nearby
Votivkirche (see p102). This is a great
choice for a traditional breakfast, and
it also hosts various cultural events.

10 Sigmund Freud Park
MAP K1
On a sunny day, these verdant lawns
(see p65) are inhabited by students
studying, picnicking, sunbathing and
debating the issues of the day.

Relaxing in Sigmund Freud Park

Places to Eat

1 Kim Kocht
MAP C3 ▪ Währinger Strasse 46
▪ 664 425 88 66 ▪ Closed Sat, Sun,
Mon D & Tue D ▪ €€€

Celebrity chef Sohyi Kim runs this
tiny, trendy venue (see p79), serving
Korean fusion cuisine with mostly
fish, seafood and vegetarian dishes.

2 Universitätsbräuhaus
MAP J1 ▪ University Campus,
Alser Strasse 4 ▪ 01 409 1815
▪ No credit cards ▪ €

Simple but tasty dishes served in
the pharmacy of the old hospital.

Chandeliered interior of Café Weimar

3 Café Weimar
MAP B2 ▪ Währinger Strasse 68
▪ 01 317 12 06 ▪ €

This traditional café-restaurant, with
a pianist, serves hot and cold snacks
and offers a set lunch at midday.

4 D'Landsknecht
MAP B3 ▪ Porzellangasse 13
▪ 01 317 43 48 ▪ €

A long-established local favourite:
expect hearty portions of traditional
Austrian soups and main dishes
at moderate prices here.

5 Gasthaus Wickerl
MAP B3 ▪ Porzellangasse 24a
▪ 01 317 74 89 ▪ Closed Sun D
▪ No credit cards ▪ €€

A traditional Viennese restaurant
with good Austrian cuisine.

PRICE CATEGORIES
For a three-course meal for one with half
a bottle of wine (or equivalent meal),
taxes and extra charges.

€ under €35   €€ €35–70   €€€ over €70

6 Oasia
MAP B4 ▪ Schlickgasse 2
▪ 01 310 01 70 ▪ Closed Sun ▪ €

Dim sum is a speciality at this
modern Asian-fusion restaurant.

7 Der Wiener Deewan
MAP C3 ▪ Liechtensteinstrasse
10 ▪ 01 925 11 85 ▪ Closed Sun &
public hols ▪ €€

The Pakistani menu served here
has garnered rave reviews.

8 Suppenwirtschaft
MAP B3 ▪ Servitengasse 6
▪ 01 317 67 45 ▪ Closed D, Sat, Sun &
public hols ▪ €

This vegan-friendly restaurant offers
a seasonal menu of soups, salads
and curries. Takeaway is the norm
here, as the seating area is small.

9 Ragusa
MAP B3 ▪ Berggasse 15
▪ 01 317 15 77 ▪ Closed Sun ▪ €€

Dalmatian cooking (specialities
include fish and seafood) in a cosy
atmosphere with outdoor seating.

10 Stomach
MAP B3 ▪ Seegasse 26 ▪ 01
310 20 99 ▪ Closed Mon & Tue ▪ €€

Enjoy modern food in one of the
nicest outdoor dining areas.

Stomach's pretty outdoor courtyard

See map on p100

🔟 MuseumsQuartier, Town Hall and Neubau

The areas around the MuseumsQuartier, Town Hall and Neubau represent both the political centre of Austria and the cultural heart of the capital, being home to a mix of government bureaus, world-class exhibition spaces and funky, Bohemian boutiques in lively, character-packed cobbled streets. This is where conventional Vienna and the city's edgier, arty side meet among restaurants, shops, vintage stores, museums and galleries.

Statues outside the Parliament building

MUSEUMSQUARTIER, TOWN HALL AND NEUBAU

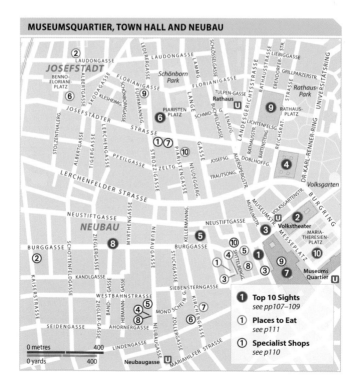

1 Top 10 Sights
see pp107–109

1 Places to Eat
see p111

1 Specialist Shops
see p110

0 metres 400
0 yards 400

1 Spittelberg
MAP J5

The charming Spittelberg area consists of a few cobbled, narrow streets with pretty houses and spouting fountains between Breite Gasse, Siebensterngasse, Sigmundsgasse and Burggasse. In the 18th century the area was full of hovels, gambling dens and brothels, but by the 19th century these had been closed down and, over time, the district became increasingly derelict. The city authorities only began to recognize the area's charm in the 1970s, and today it's a thriving enclave of galleries, handicraft shops and cosy pubs.

2 Naturhistorisches Museum
MAP K4 ▪ Maria-Theresienplatz ▪ Open 9am–6:30pm Wed–Mon (until 9pm Wed); rooftop tours in English 3pm Sun ▪ Adm (free for under 19s) ▪ www.nhm-wien.ac.at

Often voted among the world's top ten museums and built as a mirror image of its more famous neighbour, the Kunsthistorisches Museum, the Natural History Museum opened in 1889. The collections of archaeology, natural history and geology grew out of Emperor Franz Stephan's 1748 collection of natural curiosities. The museum's interior was designed to enhance the exhibits, which number more than 20 million. The most precious rarities are the 25,000-year-old Venus of Willendorf figurine and a "bouquet of jewels" given to Francis I by his wife Maria Theresa.

Naturhistorisches Museum exhibits

Lavish interior of the Volkstheater

3 Volkstheater
MAP J4 ▪ Arthur-Schnitzler-Platz 1 ▪ www.volkstheater.at

The Volkstheater ("people's theatre") was established in 1889 as a counterpart to the imperial Burgtheater (see p93). Its aim was to offer classic and modern drama to a larger audience at reasonable prices. Constructed by the acclaimed architects Ferdinand Fellner and Hermann Helmer, this theatre was designed in Historicist style and fitted with the latest technology of the time, such as electric lighting. With just under 1,000 seats, it is among the largest German-language theatres in the world.

4 Parliament
MAP K3 ▪ Dr-Karl-Renner-Ring 3 ▪ Interior closed to the public due to extensive renovation

This building (1873–83) was designed by the architect Theophil von Hansen in Greek style to celebrate the cradle of democracy. Two ramps lined by statues of Greek philosophers lead to the main entrance. The first Austrian Republic was declared here in 1918.

5 Sankt-Ulrichs-Platz
MAP E2

At the heart of this charming cobbled square is St Ulrich's church, which is surrounded by a pretty ensemble of patrician houses dating back to various periods. At No. 5 is a rare example of a Renaissance house, while the Baroque edifice at No. 27 bears a statue of St Nepomuk, who gave the house its name. During the Turkish Siege of 1683, Kara Mustafa's troops pitched their tents on this square.

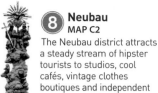

Sculpture outside St Ulrich's church

6 Piaristenkirche Maria Treu
MAP D2 ■ Jodok Fink Platz ■ Open during church services ■ www.mariatreu.at

Walking into narrow Piaristengasse from Josefstädter Strasse, the charming square on the left comes as a surprise. The Piaristenkirche Maria Treu (Maria Treu Church) here was built from 1719 onwards to a design by Lukas von Hildebrandt. The dome's frescoes are by the Austrian Baroque artist Franz Anton Maulbertsch (1752). The column in front of the church was installed in 1713 to give thanks for the end of a plague epidemic.

7 MuseumsQuartier
The former imperial stables have been imaginatively transformed into a vast complex of museums and entertainment venues (see pp34–5) that shouldn't be missed.

8 Neubau
MAP C2

The Neubau district attracts a steady stream of hipster tourists to studios, cool cafés, vintage clothes boutiques and independent stores. In the last decade, Neubau's arty, progressive character has emerged as "Vienna's Berlin". A leisurely stroll around the galleries and kooky outlets in its back-streets allows visitors a chance to experience the city's alternative side. An eclectic mish-mash of shops sells everything from modern textiles, eco-fashion bespoke jewellery and fetish gear to gourmet foods, bizarre kitchen gadgets, photographic art and multicoloured retro frocks. Fanning north from the Mariahilfer Strasse towards the Lerchenfelder Strasse, Neubau's stores run along Neubaugasse and Lindengasse. The MuseumsQuartier marks the district's eastern border.

9 Neues Rathaus
MAP J2 ■ Friedrich-Schmidt-Platz 1 ■ Tours with audio guides in English 1pm Mon, Wed & Fri ■ www.wien.gv.at

The Neo-Gothic town hall, with its spires, loggias and stone rosettes in the pointed windows, was built by Friedrich von Schmidt in 1883 to express the inhabitants' pride in their city at that time. The impressive building has seven arcaded courtyards

and 1,575 rooms, where the Vienna City Council and the mayor have their offices. All year round, various festivals take place on the square in front of the Rathaus, ranging from a Christmas market to a music film festival in summer *(see pp86–7)*. The building's façade is spectacularly highlighted at night by floodlights.

Kunsthistorisches Museum painting

⑩ Kunsthistorisches Museum

Vienna's Kunsthistorisches Museum *(see pp22–5)* is home to an impressive collection of artistic treasures, spanning the centuries from the ancient world to the modern day.

RINGSTRASSE

The Ringstrasse encircles the city's first district and is one of the world's most elegant avenues. In 1857 Franz Joseph I ordered Vienna's medieval strongholds be torn down and the city be given an imperial face with grand edifices. Palaces were then built along the new boulevard that was officially opened in 1865.

The MuseumsQuartier at night

A WALK AROUND THE MUSEUMSQUARTIER

▶ **MORNING**

Begin your day at the **Neues Rathaus**, then stroll along the Ringstrasse towards **Parliament** *(see p107)*. Once you have taken in these political gems, you can then explore the city's wonderful museums.

The museum highlights are the **Kunsthistorisches Museum** and **Naturhistorisches Museum** *(see p107)*, and you could easily spend a full day in each of these places, so be sure to select your main areas of interest and concentrate on those collections. Enjoy your morning coffee in the museums themselves – the cafés in both are excellent and offer a great view of the museums' lower floors.

Walk across the square to the **MuseumsQuartier** and wander around the many courtyards. Before embarking on another museum, stop for lunch in any of the four restaurants in the complex – all of them offer equally delicious food.

AFTERNOON

After lunch, visit **mumok** *(see p34)* and the **Leopold Museum** *(see p35)*, before leaving the complex through gates 6 or 7. These lead you straight to the **Volkstheater** *(see p107)*. Make your way up Burggasse and the **Spittelberg** area *(see p107)* spills out to your left, where you can look around the shops and galleries.

After dark, return to the Neues Rathaus to see it lit up against the night sky.

See map on p106 ←

Specialist Shops

1 Quendler's feine Weine
MAP D2 ■ Josefstädter Strasse 33 ■ www.quendler.at

This is the top address in Vienna for fine red and white Austrian wines, as well as wines from around the world.

2 Grand Cru
MAP E2 ■ Kaiserstrasse 67 ■ www.grandcru.at

Choose from a great selection of coffees, as well as delicious chocolates with various tasty fillings here.

Tasty wares on display at Grand Cru

3 Teehaus Artee
MAP E2 ■ Siebensterngasse 4 ■ www.artee.at

Offering a range of teas along with stylish teapots and cups, Artee is an elegant spot to buy and sample tea. Asian food is also served here.

4 Ina Kent Store
MAP E2 ■ Neubaugasse 34 ■ www.inakent.com

A specialist in leather goods, including handbags, this store also hosts changing exhibitions in the shop.

Stylish furniture at Das Möbel

5 Mastnak
MAP E2 ■ Neubaugasse 31 ■ www.mastnak.at

One of two shops, stocking everything from drawing pencils to schoolbags and wrapping paper. It also does printing and copying.

6 Geschirr Niessner
MAP E2 ■ Kirchengasse 9A ■ www.porzellan-wien.at

This kitchen equipment emporium has plenty of vintage products, such as English and Austrian porcelain.

7 Vinoe
MAP D2 ■ Piaristengasse 35 ■ www.vinoe.at

The specialist in wines from Lower Austria stocks 400 varieties.

8 Shu!
MAP E2 ■ Neubaugasse 34 ■ www.shu.at

Designer shoes in unusual colours, with extraordinary heels or bizarre buckles: Shu! is a footwear paradise.

9 Komische Künste
MAP K5 ■ Museumsplatz 1 ■ www.komischekuenste.com

An ideal place for lovers of cartoons and comic books. The store also has more "serious" academic works on the anatomy of the funny bone.

10 Das Möbel
MAP E2 ■ Burggasse 10 ■ cafe.dasmoebel.at

A mixture between a furniture gallery, café and restaurant where you can test out and shop for furniture while having a drink or a meal.

Places to Eat

1 Amerling Beisl
MAP E2 ▪ Stiftgasse 8 ▪ 01 526 16 60 ▪ €

This Biedermeier-style courtyard garden, open in summer, serves Viennese comfort food, including noodles and dumplings.

2 Die Wäscherei
MAP C1 ▪ Albertgasse 49 ▪ 01 409 23 75 11 ▪ €

This former laundry (see p78) is one of the hot spots in the area. It has a delicious brunch menu at weekends, but book ahead – it's very popular.

3 Plutzer Bräu
MAP E2 ▪ Schrankgasse 2 ▪ 01 526 12 15 ▪ €

A pub serving burgers, with huge TV screens for sports fans. In summer there is seating outside.

4 Tian Bistro
MAP E2 ▪ Schrankgasse 4 ▪ 01 526 94 91 ▪ €€

The shaded gardens here provide respite on hot days and it's an oasis for vegetarians in meat-eating Vienna.

5 Zu ebener Erde und erster Stock
MAP E2 ▪ Burggasse 13 ▪ 01 523 62 54 ▪ Closed Sat & Sun ▪ €€

On the ground and first floors of a Biedermeier-style house, this restaurant serves creative and traditional Austrian cuisine and fine wines.

6 Prinz Ferdinand
MAP D1 ▪ Bennoplatz 2 ▪ 01 402 94 17 ▪ €€

A typical Viennese restaurant with classic Austrian specialities. In summer there is romantic seating underneath trees on the square.

7 Figar
MAP E2 ▪ Kirchengasse 18 ▪ 01 890 99 47 ▪ Closed Thu ▪ €

Excellent brunches and several vegetarian choices are offered here. Figar is something of a hipster hangout. It is open until 2am and there is a pleasant outdoor patio in summer.

8 Witwe Bolte
MAP J5 ▪ Gutenberggasse 13 ▪ 01 523 14 50 ▪ Closed L Mon–Fri ▪ €€

This cosy spot in the Spittelberg area has outdoor seating in summer, a delightful interior and offers refined Viennese cuisine and Austrian wines.

Charming interior of Tunnel

9 Tunnel
MAP D1 ▪ Florianigasse 39 ▪ 01 405 34 65 ▪ No credit cards ▪ €

A mix of international food and plenty of Asian dishes feature on the menu here. In the evenings, there is live music until it closes at 2am.

10 Ilija
MAP D2 ▪ Piaristengasse 36 ▪ 01 408 54 31 ▪ Closed Sun ▪ €€

Cosy Croatian restaurant serves seasonal dishes, fish and other specialities from the Dalmatian Coast.

See map on p106

🔟 Opera and Naschmarkt

This is a multifaceted area, which features a variety of architectural landmarks standing regally alongside the colourful activity of the Naschmarkt. It is characterized by great buildings of various styles such as the historic State Opera House and the Academy of Fine Arts, as well as the finest examples of Viennese Art Nouveau with the Secession Building and two stunning Otto Wagner houses on Linke Wienzeile. The area is also a shoppers' paradise – Mariahilfer Strasse has hundreds of stores and many cafés and restaurants, while the Naschmarkt offers a different kind of retail experience. The lively market bears some resemblance to Middle Eastern bazaars and is a delight for all the senses.

Detail from interior of the Theater an der Wien

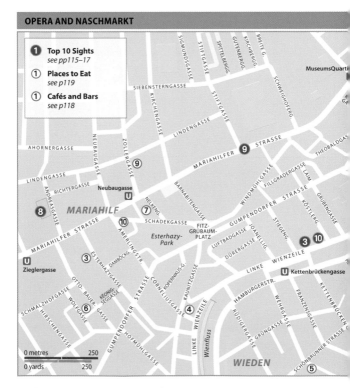

OPERA AND NASCHMARKT

1 **Top 10 Sights**
   see pp115–17

1 **Places to Eat**
   see p119

1 **Cafés and Bars**
   see p118

0 metres 250
0 yards 250

Grand staircase at the Staatsoper

1 Staatsoper

The Vienna State Opera House *(see pp36–7)* is an iconic landmark in a city that is passionate about its music. Its 300 performances a year attract an international audience, as does the annual Opera Ball, during which audience members are allowed backstage to mingle with the stars.

2 Akademie der bildenden Künste Art Collections

MAP L6 ▪ Schillerplatz 3 ▪ Open 10am–6pm Tue–Sun ▪ Adm (under 19s free) ▪ www.kunstsammlungen akademie.at

The Academy of Fine Arts Vienna, *(see p58)* designed by Theophil Hansen, occupies an elegant Italian Renaissance style Ringstrasse building. Completed in 1876, it possesses outstanding collections of paintings, with works by Titian, Rembrandt, Rubens and Hieronymus Bosch, and graphic art. Reflecting its location in a modern art school, the Art Collections regularly exhibit selected masterpieces in thought-provoking combination with international contemporary art.

3 Majolika Haus

MAP F3 ▪ Linke Wienzeile 40

One of the finest examples of an Art Nouveau-style house was designed by the celebrated architect Otto Wagner in 1898. The house is decorated with colourful floral patterns on glazed tiles – pink roses, green leaves and blue blossoms spread across the building's surface. The house is now divided into apartments with shops on the ground floor.

4 Secession Building

This late-19th-century building *(see pp38–9)* is a remarkable celebration of the Secessionist artistic movement founded by Gustav Klimt.

Vienna Secession Building's exterior

5 Naschmarkt

MAP F4 ■ Between Karlsplatz and Kettenbrückengasse ■ Open 6am–7:30pm Mon–Fri (until 5pm Sat) ■ www.naschmarkt-vienna.com

The city's largest market, bustling Naschmarkt is a colourful place with more than 100 stalls. At 6am, vendors selling fruit, vegetables, flowers, meat and fish open their stalls. On Saturdays, farmers from outside the city offer their produce, and at the Saturday flea market stalls sell everything from antiques to second-hand clothing.

6 Theater an der Wien

MAP F3 ■ Linke Wienzeile 6 ■ 01 588 30 10 10 ■ Backstage tours can be pre-booked ■ www.theater-wien.at

Emanuel Schikaneder, a friend of Mozart, founded this theatre in 1801. It remained closed for many years, until it opened its doors once again in 2006 on Mozart's 250th birth anniversary. Now billed as "The New Opera House of Vienna", it stages an opera premiere every month. There is a youthful repertory company and a programme of song

The Schiller monument

and youth opera called the Kammeroper or Chamber Opera. Performances of Mozart are frequent, but contemporary opera is also featured here.

7 Schiller Monument

MAP L6 ■ Schillerplatz

The main focal point of Schillerplatz, the charming square situated right in front of the Academy of Fine Arts, is the statue of the poet and dramatist Friedrich Schiller, sculpted in 1876 by Johannes Schilling. Opposite to it is the Goethe monument *(see p54)*, created by Edmund von Hellmer in 1900 as a tribute to another great German-language writer.

A MUSICAL CITY

Vienna is inextricably connected with classical music and often referred to as the world's musical capital. The art-loving Habsburgs acted as paymasters and provided the perfect setting for a thriving musical landscape, particularly from the late 18th to the 19th centuries. Today the traditions of its past remain, but there is also a vivid scene of contemporary music in the city.

The opulent gilded interior of the Theater an der Wien

⑧ Hofmobiliendepot
MAP F1 ■ Andreasgasse 7
■ Open 10am–6pm Tue–Sun ■ Adm
■ www.hofmobiliendepot.at

In the Imperial Furniture Collection, established in the late 18th century by Empress Maria Theresa, all the Habsburgs' furniture was stored, repaired and kept in a good state to be distributed to imperial house-holds when required. Today, the museum tells how imperial families used to live and has thousands of exhibits – from the everyday to the highly unusual – spanning more than five centuries.

Shoppers in the Mariahilfer Strasse

⑨ Mariahilfer Strasse
MAP K6

After Kärntner Strasse and the Graben, this pedestrianized street is Vienna's trendiest and busiest shop-ping mile. Hundreds of shops and a few department stores offer fashion, books, music and electronic goods, while cafés, restaurants, ice-cream parlours and cinemas abound.

⑩ Wagner Haus
MAP F3 ■ Linke Wienzeile 38

Next to the Majolika Haus is another of Otto Wagner's Art Nouveau-style buildings. The six-storey house has a white plastered façade with golden stucco elements. Between the top row of windows are golden medal-lions with female heads, designed by Koloman Moser (1868–1918). Peacock feathers trail under the medallions reaching down to the windows below. Above the rounded corner with an iron-and-glass porch are statues of female "callers" by Othmar Schimkowitz (1864–1947).

A DAY IN THE OPERA AND NASCHMARKT AREA

▶ **MORNING**

Start off by admiring the majestic, Neo-Renaissance **Staatsoper** *(see pp36–7)* and cut your way through Operngasse toward the **Secession Building** *(see pp38–9)*. You could stare at the beautiful exterior of Olbrich's Secessionist master-piece, with its ornate dome made up of gilt laurel leaves, for hours, but the stunning *Beethoven Frieze* inside this Art Nouveau building shouldn't be missed.

For a coffee and snack break, head to the historic **Café Museum** *(see p118)*, first designed by Adolf Loos in 1899.

Walk towards **Naschmarkt**, and roam the market with its variety of stalls and lively atmosphere, casting a glance over the road to the **Theater an der Wien**, the **Majolika Haus** *(see p115)* and the **Wagner Haus**.

For lunch, choose from one of the many cafés or restaurants on Naschmarkt, such as the bustling **Do An** *(see p119)*.

AFTERNOON

Make your way up to **Mariahilfer Strasse** and spend the rest of the afternoon leisurely looking around the many shops.

Stay in the area for the evening and attend a classical opera per-formance, either in the **Theater an der Wien** or in the **Staatsoper**. But, whichever of the two enter-tainment venues you choose, make sure you have booked your tickets in advance.

See map on pp114–15

Cafés and Bars

1 Café Drechsler
MAP F2 ▪ Linke Wienzeile 22
▪ www.drechsler-wien.at
Elegantly remodelled by British architects Conran & Partners, this legendary coffee house has regained its mantle as the best place for a late-night drink or an early breakfast.

2 Café Sperl
MAP K6
▪ Gumpendorfer
Strasse 11 ▪ www.cafe
sperl.at

Croissant at the Café Museum

This stylish café *(see p77)* has been in business since the 19th century and has always had a reputation for being the haunt of artists, musicians, actors and nobles.

3 Barfly's Club
MAP F2 ▪ Esterhazygasse 33
▪ www.barflys.at
Situated in the Hotel Fürst Metternich, this fashionable bar serves a huge selection of cocktails, whiskies and rums, which complement the regular live jazz and swing music.

4 Wein & Co Bar
MAP L6 ▪ Linke Wienzeile 4
▪ www.weinco.at
Right by the Secession Building, this trendy place is a wine shop cum bar with more than 60 wines from across the globe. It also serves Italian fare.

Chic interior of Wein & Co Bar

5 Naschmarkt Deli
MAP F4 ▪ Naschmarkt stall
421–36 ▪ www.naschmarkt-deli.at
This little café set amid the bustling Naschmarkt market stalls serves excellent breakfasts all day long and offers all kinds of cuisines, from Viennese to Turkish.

6 Café Museum
MAP M5 ▪ Opern-gasse 7 ▪ www.cafe museum.at
Adolf Loos's minimalist-designed coffee house *(see p76)* makes a great place to people-watch while enjoying coffee and delicious cakes.

7 Tanzcafé Jenseits
MAP F2 ▪ Nelkengasse 3
▪ www.tanzcafe-jenseits.com
An intimate little bar with plush reddish decor, which gives it a slightly faded, Hollywood-of-yesteryear feel. There is also a small dance floor.

8 Der Hannes
MAP F3 ▪ Pressgasse 29
▪ www.derhannes.at
Close to the colourful Naschmarkt, this cosy venue offers late breakfasts, pancakes with a variety of toppings and fillings, and excellent beers.

9 Café Europa
MAP E2 ▪ Zollergasse 8
▪ www.cafeeuropa.at
This spot *(see p76)* is as close as you'll come to an all-night American diner in Vienna, both in its ambience and its extensive menu. Sip on flavourful drinks and tuck into hearty food.

10 Café Ritter
MAP F2 ▪ Mariahilfer Strasse 73
▪ www.caferitter.at
A traditional café just off the main shopping drag, Ritter offers the obligatory variety of coffees, cakes, snacks and newspapers. It makes a great break from nearby shopping.

Places to Eat

(1) Umarfisch
MAP F3 ▪ Naschmarkt Stand 76–9 ▪ 01 587 04 56 ▪ Closed Sun ▪ €€

Try a seafood platter or the delicious oysters with a glass of sparkling wine at this fish restaurant.

(2) Theatercafé
MAP F3 ▪ Linke Wienzeile 6 ▪ 01 585 62 62 ▪ Closed Sun ▪ €€

Serving Austrian food with Asian and Italian influences, this place is busy after shows at the theatre next door.

PRICE CATEGORIES

For a three-course meal for one with half a bottle of wine (or equivalent meal), taxes and extra charges.

€ under €35   €€ €35–70   €€€ over €70

(6) Steman
MAP F1 ▪ Otto-Bauer Gasse 7 ▪ 01 597 85 09 ▪ Closed Sat & Sun ▪ No credit cards ▪ €€

Enjoy a pre-booked wine tasting or dine at long tables at this cosy part-wooden-panelled place (see p79) serving traditional Viennese fare.

(7) Indian Pavilion
MAP F3 ▪ Naschmarkt 74–5 ▪ 01 587 85 61 ▪ Closed D & Sun ▪ €

Vienna's smallest Indian restaurant is also its best. Try the lentil soup, then the divine mango pickle with a curry. Get there early as it fills up quickly.

Colourful exterior of Do An at night

(3) Do An
MAP F4 ▪ Naschmarkt stall 412 ▪ 01 585 82 53 ▪ Closed Sun ▪ No credit cards ▪ €

Do An prepares a varied cuisine – the smoked tofu with sautéed courgettes, carrots and spring onions is delicious.

(4) Salzberg
MAP G2 ▪ Magdalenenstrasse 17 ▪ 01 581 62 26 ▪ €€

Creative Viennese dishes are paired with beer specially brewed in eastern Austria. The weekend brunch buffet here is particularly good.

(5) Zu den drei Buchteln
MAP G3 ▪ Wehrgasse 9 ▪ 01 587 83 65 ▪ Closed Sun & public hols ▪ No credit cards ▪ €€

This friendly place (see p79) serves Bohemian specialities such as yeast cakes, known as *buchteln*.

(8) Café Amarcord
MAP F3 ▪ Rechte Wienzeile 15 ▪ 01 587 47 09 ▪ Closed Sat & Sun ▪ No credit cards ▪ €€

A very relaxed place (open until 1am) with leather sofas – perfect after the hectic Naschmarkt. The food is tasty and there is a wide range of choices.

(9) Restaurant Sopile
MAP F4 ▪ Paulanergasse 10 ▪ 01 585 24 33 ▪ Closed L, Sun & public hols ▪ €€

An Istrian restaurant with a strong emphasis on fish dishes as well as truffles and game. Excellent wine list.

(10) Chang
MAP F4 ▪ Waaggasse 1 ▪ 01 961 92 12 ▪ Closed Sun ▪ €€

Simple, reasonably-priced Asian food is served at this modern noodle bar. Try the weekly lunchtime set menus.

See map on pp114–15 ←

🔟 From Karlskirche to the Belvedere

The area from Karlskirche to the Belvedere Palace is filled with grand mansions and summer residences from the 18th and 19th centuries. Vienna's aristocracy built their summer palaces here

because it was in the countryside but not too far from the city. Prince Eugene's summer retreat, the Belvedere, dominates the area, but there are several other ornate homes, such as the Palais Schwarzenberg and the Palais Hoyos, which are well worth a visit. Today many such buildings are embassies and some of the once private gardens are public parks. During Roman times the civil settlement of the Vindobona military camp was situated here. The area's main roads, Landstrasser Hauptstrasse and Rennweg, follow old Roman routes.

Painted dome inside the Salesianerinnenkirche

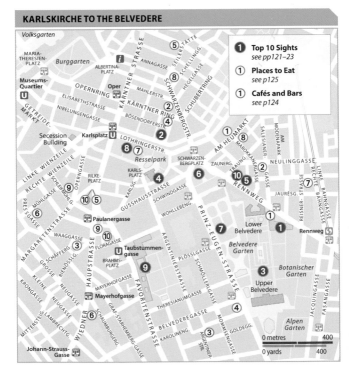

KARLSKIRCHE TO THE BELVEDERE

1 **Top 10 Sights**
see pp121–23

1 **Places to Eat**
see p125

1 **Cafés and Bars**
see p124

0 metres 400
0 yards 400

1 Salesianerinnenkirche
MAP F6 ■ Rennweg 8–10
■ **Open only for services 7am Mon–Sat, 9am Sun**

Amalia Wilhelmina (1673–1742), the widow of Emperor Joseph I, founded this monastery of the Salesian order in 1717 in thanks for her recovery from smallpox. The architect Donato Felice d'Allio completed the complex with its eight large courtyards in 1728. Along with the Belvedere and Palais Schwarzenberg, it forms a magnificent Baroque ensemble. The dome is decorated with frescoes by the Rococo painter Antonio Pellegrini (1675–1741) showing the Virgin Mary's ascension to heaven. According to Amalia Wilhelmina's will, her body is buried under the high altar, but an urn with her heart was placed inside her husband's coffin in the imperial crypt on Neuer Markt.

Inside the Musikverein's Golden Hall

2 Musikverein
MAP N6 ■ Musikvereinsplatzl
■ **01 505 81 90** ■ **Adm** ■ **www.musikverein.at**

This impressive concert hall (see p72) in Greek Renaissance style was built by Theophil von Hansen in 1869 for the Society of Friends of Music. It became famous after the Vienna Philharmonic Orchestra began giving their annual New Year's Concert here in 1941. There are three performance areas, but the main auditorium, the Golden Hall, is the finest, with lavish decorations and great acoustics. Call ahead to book guided tours.

3 The Belvedere
These two 18th-century palace buildings (see pp28–31) are linked by landscaped gardens, featuring tiered fountains and cascades, with statues of nymphs.

4 Karlskirche
This Baroque masterpiece is one of Vienna's most impressive churches (see pp32–3), with its beautiful carved columns and green dome.

Karlskirche exterior

OTTO WAGNER

Before Otto Wagner (1841–1918) became one of Vienna's most eminent architects and an advocate of functional architecture, he was a Classical Revivalist. He moved from the Neo-Renaissance style to modernity by rejecting brick for steel structures. No other architect has left such a strong imprint on the city.

5 Gardekirche
MAP F5 ■ Rennweg 5a

The construction of this Rococo church was decreed by Empress Maria Theresa in 1755, and her favourite architect Nikolaus von Pacassi (1716–90) completed the building in 1763. The plain, cubic structure with a red tiled roof and a green cupola was the church to the nearby military hospital. The interior is decorated with elaborate stucco work, and behind the high altar is the painting *Christ on the Crucifix* by Peter Strudel, the founder of Vienna's first art school. The church has been the Polish national church in Vienna since 1897.

6 Liberation Monument
MAP F5 ■ Schwarzenbergplatz

This monument to the Soviet Red Army is a reminder of Vienna's postwar history, when the city was occupied by the four Allied powers and divided into four zones. Schwarzenbergplatz was part of the Soviet zone and renamed Stalinplatz. The monument was installed in 1945 and, at the end of Allied occupation in 1955, the republic pledged to keep and maintain the monument.

7 Schwarzenberggarten
MAP F5 ■ Schwarzenbergplatz 9
■ Closed to the public

In 1697, the noted Baroque architect Lukas von Hildebrandt was commissioned to build a summer palace here, which was purchased by the influential Schwarzenberg family in 1720. Architects Johann Bernhard Fischer von Erlach and his son Josef Emanuel continued adorning the palace and laid out the garden in formal French style.

8 Otto Wagner Pavilion
MAP F4 ■ Karlsplatz
■ Exhibition: open Apr–Oct 10am–6pm Tue–Sun (closed public hols)
■ Adm (under 19s free)

The two pavilions on Karlsplatz were built by Otto Wagner in 1897 as twin stations for the Vienna City Train, the horse-drawn and later steam-powered predecessors of today's underground rail system. In total, Wagner designed 34 stations and various bridges and viaducts for

Liberation Monument

Inside the Otto Wagner Pavilion

A DAY'S WALK FROM KARLSPLATZ TO THE BELVEDERE

the train line that was finished in 1901. The pavilions on Karlsplatz are made of steel and marble slabs, and the roof over the arched gate is decorated with golden ornaments. Both stations became obsolete once the modern underground lines had been built. Today the Otto Wagner Pavilion is used by the Wien Museum and the other station is a café (see p124).

Theresianum
MAP G4 ■ Favoritenstrasse 15
■ Closed to the public

On the site of this elite private school once stood an imperial summer palace, until it was destroyed by Turkish troops in 1683. On its ruins the Italian architect Lodovico Burnacini built the Theresianum (1687–90). Comprising a long building with a sober façade, it was named after Empress Maria Theresa, who installed an educational institute here for the young nobility. Today it is a top private school and a diplomatic academy.

Palais Hoyos
MAP F5 ■ Rennweg 3
■ Closed to the public

The renowned Otto Wagner built this Neo-Renaissance palace as his home in 1891, before he joined the Vienna Secessionist movement. The windows of the upper floor are framed with intricate floral details, but the ground and first floors are built in sombre pale stone.

▶ MORNING

Start your day at Karlsplatz, where you can inspect the **Otto Wagner Pavilion** in Resselpark and then walk on to the splendid **Karlskirche** (see pp32–3). Left of the church is the **Wien Museum Karlsplatz** (see p57), a great place to spend an hour or two studying the city's history. Don't miss the Klimt and Schiele paintings, as well as Adolf Loos's original living room from 1903.

Head towards Argentinierstrasse, right of Karlskirche as you face away from the church, where you can enjoy some coffee and cake in **Café Goldegg** (see p124).

Walk east to the **Liberation Monument**, then take Rennweg and pass by Otto Wagner's **Palais Hoyos**. For lunch, pop into **Salm Bräu** (see p124).

AFTERNOON

Head for the **Belvedere** (see pp28–31), where you could easily spend the rest of the day. After having a look around the exhibition in the **Lower Belvedere**, walk through the formal gardens towards the **Upper Belvedere**, home to the Austrian National Gallery with many Klimt, Schiele, Gerstl and Attersee paintings. You can also visit the **Belvedere 21** gallery (see p29), located about ten minutes' walk from here on Arsenalstrasse 1. It holds changing exhibitions of Austrian art from 1945 to the present day.

Consider attending a concert in the **Konzerthaus** (see p73) or the **Musikverein** (see p121), but you need to book a day in advance.

See map on p120 ←

Cafés and Bars

Traditional dining area of Salm Bräu

1 Salm Bräu
MAP F5 ■ Rennweg 8
■ www.salmbraeu.com

Hearty dishes are complemented by beers brewed-in house at Salm Bräu. Try the different sausage specialities and bread with various options.

2 Café Schwarzenberg
MAP N6 ■ Kärntner Ring 17
■ www.cafe-schwarzenberg.at

A traditional café with plush interiors, this spot offers outdoor seating on its terrace in the summer. It also hosts jazz breakfasts and changing exhibitions of Viennese artists. Thursday through Sunday, evenings come alive with fantastic piano concerts.

3 Café Goldegg
MAP H5 ■ Argentinierstrasse 49/corner of Goldeggasse ■ www.cafegoldegg.at

A peaceful café and a retreat for reading, Goldegg also has a games room where you can play chess or cards.

4 Café Imperial
MAP N6 ■ Kärntner Ring 16
■ www.cafe-imperial.at

This historic café opened in 1873 for the Universal Exhibition and is based in the former residence of the Prince of Württemberg. Enjoy a cup of coffee paired with the café's signature tortes.

5 Silver Bar at the Hotel Das Triest
MAP F4 ■ Wiedner Hauptstrasse 12
■ www.dastriest.at

With its cool, laid-back vibe and first-class cocktails, the Silver Bar has long been the choice of Vienna's hip crowd. Enjoy a relaxed drink in its opulent surroundings.

6 Café Wortner
MAP G4
■ Wiedner Hauptstrasse 55 ■ www.wortner.at

A great historic coffee house with a whiff of the Biedermeier era about it; it's especially good for sitting outside.

7 Café Karl-Otto
MAP F4 ■ Otto Wagner Pavilion, Karlsplatz ■ www.jugendstil-cafe.at

Karl-Otto is a popular café-restaurant serving traditional Viennese food by day, and a club with international DJs spinning lively tracks by night.

8 Flanagan's Irish Pub
MAP N5 ■ Schwarzenbergstrasse 1–3 ■ www.flanagans.at

Enjoy a few pints of Guinness in a traditional Irish pub setting. The furniture was imported from Cork.

9 Point of Sale
MAP F4 ■ Schleifmühlgasse 12
■ www.thepointofsale.at

This modern designer café serves international breakfasts, snacks and tarts until late into the afternoon.

10 Artner auf der Wieden
MAP G4 ■ Floragasse 6
■ www.artner.co.at

A cosy wine bar and restaurant. Try the homemade goat's cheese marinated in olive oil and herbs. You can also take a bottle home with you from the wine boutique.

See map on p120

Places to Eat

PRICE CATEGORIES
For a three-course meal for one with half a bottle of wine (or equivalent meal), taxes and extra charges.

€ under €35   €€ €35–70   €€€ over €70

1 EssDur
MAP P6 ■ Am Heumarkt 6
■ 01 512 55 50 ■ €€
Enjoy a pre-concert evening meal at EssDur, the in-house restaurant *(see p79)* of the magnificent Konzerthaus.

2 Santa Lucia
MAP F6 ■ Salesianergasse 10
■ 01 714 21 63 ■ €
Vienna's only Italian/Indian restaurant is a favourite with locals. There's free tiramisu with every dinner.

3 Wieden Bräu
MAP G4 ■ Waaggasse 5
■ 01 586 03 00 ■ €
This beerhall and beer garden serves Viennese food and has a brewery that offers tours and makes its own beer.

4 Art Corner
MAP G5 ■ Prinz-Eugen-Straße 56/1 ■ 01 505 18 21 ■ €€
Located close to The Belvedere, Art Corner is a traditional Greek restaurant with alfresco dining. The owner will give you a warm welcome.

5 Ribs of Vienna
MAP N4 ■ Weihburggasse 22
■ 01 513 85 19 ■ €€
In a narrow room with bench tables in a vaulted basement dating to 1591, try the popular "one-metre spareribs".

6 Gasthaus Ubl
MAP F3 ■ Pressgasse 26
■ 01 587 64 37 ■ Closed Mon & Tue
■ No credit cards ■ €
Probably Vienna's last simply styled *gasthaus*, this is the perfect place for dinner. Classic Viennese food is served in oak-panelled surroundings.

7 Zur Steirischen Botschaft
MAP F6 ■ Strohgasse 11 ■ 01 712 33 67 ■ Closed Sat, Sun & public hols ■ €€
Dishes from Austria's southern province of Styria are served in this restaurant with a lovely garden.

8 Gmoa Keller
MAP P6 ■ Am Heumarkt 25
■ 01 712 53 10 ■ Closed Sun & public hols ■ €€
Favoured by musicians from the concert halls nearby, this place is known for its schnitzels, seasonal dishes and wines.

9 Wiener Wirtschaft
MAP G4 ■ Wiedner Hauptstrasse 27–29 ■ 01 22 111 364 ■ €€
A short walk away from Karlsplatz, this restaurant serves Austrian dishes, and its speciality, gulash.

10 Bistro Porto
MAP F4 ■ Wiedner Hauptstrasse 12 ■ 01 589 18 0 ■ Closed Sun ■ €€€
Fine Italian cooking is served in an elegant setting at the Hotel Das Triest *(see p142)*.

Bistro Porto's smart dining room

TOP 10 Greater Vienna

Horse heads on the wall of Hermesvilla stables

The city of Vienna is located where the hills of the Vienna Woods slope down into the Wiener Becken (the Vienna basin); from here the city spreads out on both sides of the Danube. The woods provide a welcome green belt and a recreation area for city dwellers. Today's suburbs, such as Grinzing and Nussdorf, were once countryside villages, until the city swallowed them up. In the 17th and 18th centuries the city's noble families built their summer residences within easy reach of the capital, but far enough out to benefit from cool rural surroundings during the hottest time of the year. Schloss Schönbrunn, Geymüllerschlössel and Hermesvilla were such examples. Also away from the centre, for reasons of hygiene and space, is the country's largest cemetery, the Zentralfriedhof.

GREATER VIENNA

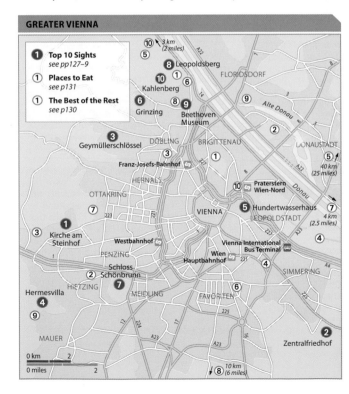

- **1** Top 10 Sights
  see pp127–9
- **1** Places to Eat
  see p131
- **1** The Best of the Rest
  see p130

Detail from the exterior of the Art Nouveau Kirche am Steinhof

1 Kirche am Steinhof

Baumgartner Höhe 1 ■ Bus 47A, 48A ■ 01 910 60 11 007 ■ Open 4–5pm Sat, noon–4pm Sun ■ Guided tours: 3pm Sat, 4pm Sun & by appt ■ Adm

This church (see p51), another masterpiece by Otto Wagner (see p122), was created between 1905 and 1907 as a place of worship for the patients at the Steinhof psychiatric hospital. The hospital complex at the edge of the Vienna Woods was designed to bring patients closer to a healthy and natural environment to help with their recovery. The church's golden dome can be seen from the Gloriette building in Schönbrunn Park.

2 Zentralfriedhof

Simmeringer Hauptstrasse 234, Tor 2 ■ Tram 6 & 71 ■ Open dawn–dusk

More than three million people have been buried in this 2.5-ha (6-acre) cemetery since it opened in 1874, among them 500 Austrian politicians, composers and actors. Max Hegele, Otto Wagner's student, designed the entrance portal, the mortuary and the Dr-Karl-Lueger-Gedächtniskirche, named after a Vienna mayor (1897–1910). The church is among Vienna's most important Art Nouveau buildings. Within the Zentralfriedhof are separate burial areas for followers of different faiths.

3 Geymüllerschlössel

Pötzleinsdorferstrasse 102 ■ Open May–Dec: 11am–6pm Sat & Sun ■ Tram 41 then Bus 41A ■ 711 36 298 ■ Adm (under 19s free)

The Geymüllerschlössel is a summer palace, reflecting Biedermeier style. Owned by the Museum of Applied Arts, it houses 170 clocks, among them an early Viennese flute clock (c1800) that plays music by Haydn.

4 Hermesvilla

Lainzer Tiergarten ■ U-Bahn U4 to Heitzing; trams 60 or 62 to Hermesstrasse then bus 60B to Lainzer Tor ■ Open mid-Mar–Oct: 10am–6pm Tue–Sun & public hols ■ Adm (under 19s and every first Sun free) ■ www.wienmuseum.at

Emperor Franz Joseph had this palace built for his wife Elisabeth between 1882 and 1886 by architect Karl von Hasenauer. The Hermes statue in the park gives it the name.

The pretty Hermesvilla palace

The colourful Hundertwasserhaus

5 Hundertwasserhaus

With perhaps the most unusual and colourful private residences in the world, this apartment block *(see pp40–41)* was built in 1985 by artist Friedensreich Hundertwasser.

6 Grinzing
U-Bahn U4, U6; tram 38

Vienna is the only capital in the world where wine grapes are grown within the city boundaries – some 675 ha (1,670 acres) of vineyards are found here. The most widely known wine-growing community in the city is Grinzing. Once a small vintners' village on the outskirts of the city, it is today a hub of *heurigen (see pp80–81)*, with crowds of both locals and tourists flocking to the wine taverns. The narrow streets still have an old-fashioned rural charm.

7 Schloss Schönbrunn

This imperial Baroque palace *(see pp42–5)*, with its stunning land-scaped gardens, is one of Vienna's most visited sights.

8 Leopoldsberg
Train Nussdorf; bus 38A; U-Bahn U4 Heiligenstadt

Dominating the Danube valley is the Leopoldsberg mountain. From its peak at 425 m (1,400 ft), you get an excellent view of the entire region around Vienna. Leopoldsberg is named after the Babenberg ruler Leopold III (1073–1136) and the ruins of the 13th-century Babenberg castle destroyed by the Turks in 1529 are still visible. An older church on top of the mountain was also destroyed by the Turks and was replaced by a Baroque church in the 18th century. Next to Leopoldsberg is its slightly higher twin peak, Kahlenberg.

VIENNA WOODS

The Vienna Woods spread towards the west of the city and were turned into a protected area as early as 1467 by Emperor Friedrich III. This meant the forest was no longer endangered by road building, but by people collecting fire-wood. In the 19th century, the forest was threatened with being cut down to gain resources, but today the Vienna Woods are as popular for excursions as ever.

---

9 Beethoven Museum
Probusgasse 6 ■ U-Bahn U4, U6; Bus 38A ■ Open 10am–1pm & 2–6pm Tue–Sun ■ Adm (free for under 19s and every first Sun)

In 2017, this small house where composer Ludwig van Beethoven lived during the summer was expanded by the Wien Museum and inaugurated as the first full-scale Beethoven Museum in Vienna. The famous composer came to the

then-rural village of Heligenstäder for its healing mineral springs to gain relief for his deafness. Unfortunately nothing helped. In 1802, while he was still here, he wrote the Heiligenstädter Testament, a poignant letter to his brothers. The letter was, however, never sent.

The Danube by the Kahlenberg

⑩ Kahlenberg
U-Bahn U4 to Heiligenstadt then bus 38A

Covered with trees and vineyards, the 484-m- (1,580-ft-) high Kahlenberg mountain is on the edge of the Vienna Woods. The Höhenstrasse, a scenic route lined with trees, occasionally offers a glimpse of the city. It winds its way up from Grinzing, and it peak offers a breathtaking view of Vienna. During the Turkish siege of 1683, the Polish troops under King Jan III Sobieski descended from the top of this hill to defeat the Turkish army on 12 September that year. The little Baroque church on top of Kahlenberg commemorates this historic event.

Stunning façade of Schloss Schönbrunn

A DAY ON VIENNA'S OUTSKIRTS

▶ **MORNING**

To beat the crowds and enjoy the peace, begin your day at the magnificent former imperial summer residence **Schloss Schönbrunn** *(see pp42–5)*. You could easily spend a day in the palace, walking in the park and the formal French garden, or visiting the world's oldest zoo at Schönbrunn Park. For a relaxing drink and a great view of the palace and the city, head to the far end of the park to the coffee house in the Gloriette building.

Stroll through the park towards the Hietzinger gate of the palace. Just around the corner is the Plachutta Heitzing *(Auhofstrasse 1)*, where you can get a taste of a real *tafelspitz (see p74)* for lunch.

AFTERNOON

After lunch, head to the **Kirche am Steinhof** *(see p127)*. Take the U4 Schönbrunn U-bahn to the Unter St Veit stop, then cross the street to reach the 47A bus stop. Take the bus from here. It will pass Baumgarten cemetery en route to the Otto Wagner Hospital. From here a wooded path winds up to the church.

From Kirche am Steinhof opt to head to the leafy *heurigen* of Grinzing for a relaxing evening.

Walk north from the church on the footpath to Pönningerweg. From here the 46A bus takes you to Ottakring station. Next, take the S45 Schnellbahn train to Wien Oberdöbling Bahnhof, from where the 38 tram goes ● straight to **Grinzing**.

See map on p126 ←

The Best of the Rest

1 Nussdorf
Train Nussdorf; tram D

Nussdorf's picturesque location amid hills overgrown with vineyards is complemented by its long narrow streets.

2 Vienna International Centre
Wagramerstrasse 5 ■ U-Bahn U1 ■ Guided Tours (ID needed) 11am, 2pm & 3:30pm Mon–Fri (Jul–Aug: also 12:30pm); Donauturm: open 10am–11:30pm daily ■ Adm ■ www.unvienna.org

Also known as the UNO City, this is the Vienna headquarters of the UN. Adjacent to the complex lies the Donaupark and its iconic Donauturm.

3 Ernst Fuchs Museum
Hüttelbergstrasse 26 ■ U-Bahn U4; bus 52A, 52B ■ Open 10am–4pm Tue–Sun & by appt (call 01 914 85 75) ■ Adm ■ www.ernstfuchs museum.at

A stunning villa, built by Otto Wagner but altered later by Ernst Fuchs, whose paintings are displayed here.

4 Sankt-Marxer-Friedhof
Leberstrasse 6–8 ■ S-Bahn S1, S7; Tram 71 ■ Open 6:30am–8pm daily (Oct–Mar: until 6:30pm)

The final resting place of prominent Austrians, including Mozart.

5 Schloss Hof
Imperial Festival Palace Hof ■ Train to Marchegg, then shuttle bus ■ Open 10am–6pm daily (mid-Nov–mid-Mar: until 4pm) ■ www.schlosshof.at

This was the former country seat of Prince Eugene of Savoy and later Empress Maria Theresa.

6 Lehár-Schikaneder Schlössl
Hackhofergasse 18 ■ U-Bahn U4; S-Bahn S40; tram D ■ Open by appt (call 01 318 5416)

This Baroque palace was once home to Emanuel Schikaneder, who wrote the libretto for *The Magic Flute*, and later to composer Franz Lehár.

7 Lobau National Park
U-Bahn U1 or U2, then bus 26A or 291

The Lobau is wild national parkland, locally known as "Vienna's jungle". It features pretty lakes, secluded forests and wildlife.

8 Laxenburg
U-Bahn U1, then bus 200 ■ www.schloss-laxenburg.at

The Laxenburg palace and its park were established by Empress Maria Theresa in the 18th century.

9 Lainzer Tiergarten
1130 Vienna ■ U-Bahn Hütteldorf; U-Bahn U4 Heitzing, then bus 56B ■ Open 8am–dusk daily ■ www.lainzer-tiergarten.at

A former hunting area surrounding the Hermesvilla *(see p127)*, this is now a wildlife refuge with wild boar, deer and bighorn sheep. It has sheltered observation areas and walkways.

10 Klosterneuburg
U-Bahn U4, then bus 540

This ancient town has an impressive Augustine abbey *(see p86)* founded in the early 12th century by Babenberg ruler Leopold III.

Schloss Hof palace

Places to Eat

1 Mraz & Sohn
Wallensteinstrasse 59 ■ Tram 5, 33 ■ 01 330 45 94 ■ Closed Sat, Sun & public hols ■ €€€

The two-Michelin-starred Mraz & Sohn is one of the best restaurants in Vienna. The chef's innovative cooking can be enjoyed in a relaxed setting.

2 Café Dommayer-Oberlaa
Corner Dommayergasse/ Auhofstrasse 2 ■ U-Bahn U4 ■ 01 877 54 65 ■ €

Dommayer-Oberlaa is a traditional café with red velvet upholstery, a wooden veranda and a pretty garden. Johann Strauss used to perform here.

3 Fischer Bräu
Billrothstrasse 17 ■ U-Bahn U6; tram 37, 38 ■ 01 369 59 49 ■ No credit cards ■ €

There is a pleasant beer garden at this restaurant and pub, which has wooden interiors and its own brewery.

4 Café-Restaurant Lusthaus
Freudenau 254, end of Prater Hauptallee ■ Bus 77A ■ 01 728 95 65 ■ Closed Oct–Apr: Wed ■ €€

This octagonal pavilion in Prater park was built in 1874 as a meeting point for the imperial hunting party. It is now a charming restaurant with lovely views of the park.

5 Skyline Lounge Restaurant
Am Kahlenberg 2–3 ■ U-Bahn U4 to Heiligenstadt, then bus 38 ■ 01 328 15 00 700 ■ €€€

Apt for a special occasion, this place offers a multi-course menu that can be enjoyed on the terrace along with panoramic views of Vienna.

6 Meixner's Gastwirtschaft
Buchengasse 64 ■ U-Bahn U1 ■ 01 604 27 10 ■ Closed Sat & Sun ■ €€

Family-owned Meixner's prepares Viennese cuisine at the highest level. Be sure to sample the Austrian lamb.

Meixner's Gastwirtschaft's courtyard

7 Plachuttas Grünspan
Ottakringer Strasse 266 ■ U-Bahn U3; bus 45A, 46A; tram 46 ■ 01 480 57 30 ■ No credit cards ■ €€

Vienna's most acclaimed beer garden, with indoor seating all year round.

8 Amador
Grinzingerstrasse 86 ■ U-Bahn U4 to Heiligenstadt, then bus 38A ■ 01 660 90 70 500 ■ Closed Sat–Tue ■ €€€

Set within a vaulted cellar, this three-Michelin-starred restaurant offers daring gastronomy and superb wine.

9 La Creperie
An der Oberen Alten Donau 6 ■ U-Bahn U6 ■ 01 270 31 00 ■ €€

Open until midnight, this creperie is frequented by tourists and locals alike.

10 Geschmacks-Tempel
MAP B6 ■ Praterstrasse 56, inner courtyard ■ U-Bahn Nestroyplatz ■ 01 214 01 79 ■ Closed Mon & public hols ■ €€

Located near the house where the *Blue Danube Waltz* was penned, this restaurant offers inexpensive set lunch menus in an intimate setting.

See map on p126

Streetsmart

Getting Around

Arriving by Air

Found 19 km (12 miles) southeast of the city centre, **Vienna International Airport**, known locally as Schwechat, serves over 100 airlines. These include easyJet, British Airways and Austrian Airlines, the main Austrian carrier. Travellers from the US can fly direct to Vienna from a number of US destinations with Austrian Airlines. The airport has all the usual facilities, including restaurants, duty free shops and banks.

Taxis will take passengers to any destination in the centre for a fixed €36. Buses from Vienna Airport Lines go to all major areas for €8 (under 14s free). A non-stop City Airport Train called **CAT** offers luxury seating and a 16-minute ride to Wien Mitte train station for €12 (under 12s free). A faster alternative is the new Railjet high-speed train, which takes 15 minutes and costs €4.20, stopping at the main Hauptbahnhof railway station. There's also the S7, a slightly slower train that stops at the more centrally located Wien Mitte and Wien Praterstern stations. It takes 25 minutes to reach the former or 30 minutes to the latter, and is the same price as the Railjet.

A cheaper alternative to Vienna International Airport, Bratislava's **Milan Rastislav Štefánik Airport** in neighbouring Slovakia is less than two hours' drive from central Vienna and is better served by budget airlines.

Long-Distance Bus Travel

Vienna's main coach station, the **Vienna International Bus Terminal** (VIB), is located close to Erdberg U3 underground station. Services arrive here from most major European cities, including Berlin, London and Paris.

Postbus and **Flixbus** run routes throughout Austria and Slovakia. Coaches arrive in Vienna at the Wien Hauptbahnhof bus terminal.

Domestic/Regional Train Travel

Train travel is a fast way to get around Austria, which has an efficient high-speed network and reliable local services.

The vast majority of Austria's rail services are run by **Österreichische Bundesbahnen** (Austrian Federal Railways), which is more commonly known as ÖBB.

The fastest train, the Railjet, can travel at speeds of up to 230 km (143 miles) per hour and links the major Austrian cities, including Salzburg, Graz and Linz, as well as cities across Germany, Italy, Hungary, the Czech Republic and Switzerland. It has free access to movies and WiFi, and electrical charging stations for laptops. Slower regional trains serve smaller towns, but to reach the more off-the-beaten-track locations in the Alps you will need to change to regional local bus services.

Public Transport

Wiener Linien is Vienna's main public transport authority. Safety and hygiene measures, timetables, ticket information, transport maps and more can be obtained from Wiener Linien information and ticket offices or the Wiener Linien website. The public transport network is made up of trams (Strassenbahn), buses (Autobus) and underground trains (U-Bahn).

The city's transport system works largely on an honesty system – there are no ticket barriers at stations, allowing passengers to quickly hop on and off. However, checks by transport authority staff do take place – you'll occasionally be asked for your *Fahrschein* (ticket) by a transport guard. Travellers caught without a valid ticket will be fined €103.

Rush hour on weekdays is from about 7am to 9:30am, then again from 4:30pm to 6:30pm. Smoking is banned in stations and on public transport.

Tickets

Vienna's public transport ticketing system is less confusing than it appears at first glance. Buying a ticket in advance is usually the easiest option. Tickets are sold at newsagents *(Tabak Trafiken)*, from ticket machines at stations, or at the counters of U-Bahn and S-Bahn offices.

Vienna city is zone 100 of the Austrian regional fare system; a standard ticket covers all areas of the city and allows passengers to change trains and lines and switch from the underground to a tram or a bus, as long as they take the most direct route and don't break their journey.

Wiener Linien's **EASY CityPass** is a good value option for anyone who is planning on using public transport for more than one day. The pass is available for 24, 48 and 72 hours, or a week, and also entitles the bearer to discounts at some of the city's museums, galleries and shops.

The Wiener Linien 8-Tage-Karte (€40.80) is best for groups and consists of eight strips which, when stamped, are valid for a day.

Children under 6 may travel for free on the city's transport network, while those aged between 6 and 14 qualify for half-price single tickets. The latter can also travel free during holidays, providing they can show proof of age.

U-Bahn

Vienna's underground system (U-Bahn) is a modern, clean, fast and reliable way of crossing the city. Expansion of the system is ongoing, though this is of more interest to those who live on the fringes of the city.

The U-Bahn operates seven days a week from around 5am to 12:30am. During the day, trains depart every 5 minutes or so, though they run less frequently after about 8pm. A 24-hour service runs on weekends and public holidays. Outside these hours, the U-Bahn

service is replaced by Vienna NightLine buses.

The U-Bahn's five colour-coded lines are U1, U2, U3, U4 and U6. The U5 line is due to open in 2026. Check the Wiener Linien website for information regarding timetables, tickets and service updates. The U-Bahn is generally safe, but in case of emergencies there are help points on most platforms.

Smoking is prohibited on U-Bahn platforms and on the trains themselves. Displays above the train doors show stations and connections, and a recorded voice announces stops and also connections to trams and buses. Signs indicate where prams can be stored by the doors. Bicycles are allowed on a few train carriages, although not before 9am or between 3 and 6:30pm Monday to Friday. Be aware that doors are opened manually and can be stiff and heavy.

Tram

Vienna's tram network is one of the largest in the world, with almost 30 routes. Known locally as "Bim" for its distinctive bell sound, it is a delightful way to get around the city. For the ultimate experience, seek out one of the old, traditional models with their wooden seats and vintage interiors.

Most of the main sights in Vienna's historic centre, such as the Staatsoper, Parliament and Neues Rathaus, are located on the popular Ring Tram route. Passengers will need to purchase a Round-the-Ring ticket (€9)

for a complete unbroken journey. On-board services include audio-visual information about highlights along the route, delivered via a multi-lingual multimedia system. Ring trams depart every 30 minutes all year round, from 10am to 5:30pm.

Most trams are equipped with seats for travellers with specific requirements. However, the modern low-riding trams are a more wheelchair-friendly option. Look for vehicles with the ULF (Ultra Low Floor) sign.

DIRECTORY

ARRIVING BY AIR

CAT
W cityairporttrain.com

Milan Rastislav Štefánik Airport
W bts.aero

Vienna International Airport
W viennaairport.com

LONG-DISTANCE BUS TRAVEL

Flixbus
W flixbus.co.uk

Postbus
W postbus.at

Vienna International Bus Terminal
W vib-wien.at

DOMESTIC/REGIONAL TRAIN TRAVEL

Österreichische Bundesbahnen
W oebb.at

PUBLIC TRANSPORT

Wiener Linien
W wienerlinien.at

TICKETS

EASY CityPass
W easycitypass.com

Bus

Bus stops are marked with a green "H" for *Haltestelle*, or stop. All stops display bus numbers, destinations, timetables and route maps. Buses should stop automatically at all bus stops but if you are in any doubt whatsoever, flag it down.

Tickets purchased from the driver will be valid for one bus journey only. If you have already purchased a ticket from a newsagent or ticket machine, you will need to validate it in the ticket-stamping machine on the bus. If you have already made part of your journey by tram or by U-Bahn, there is no need to stamp your ticket again. All buses in Vienna are wheelchair-accessible.

After midnight, Vienna's night bus service takes over. These operate at 30-minute intervals until 4am. There is some variation between the services operating on weekday nights (Sunday to Thursday) and those at weekends and on public holidays. Night buses are marked by the letter "N". All night buses in Vienna start from Schwedenplatz, the Opera and Schottentor, and together serve most suburbs. Tickets can be purchased from the driver and all other prebought tickets and passes are valid.

Taxi

Taxis are a comfortable, if more expensive, way of getting around. There is a €3.40 minimum fee during the day, then €0.80 per kilometre. At night, on Sundays and on public holidays, the minimum charge is €4.30. Round the fare up to the nearest euro or 5 euros.

Taxis in Vienna are instantly recognizable by a "TAXI" sign on the roof, which will be illuminated if the vehicle is available to hail. Phone to book, or hail at a taxi stand – for Vienna-wide locations see the Vienna Taxis section on the **City of Vienna** website or download a free Vienna taxi app. Smartphone taxis now operating in Vienna include Uber, MyDriver and Blacklane.

Vienna's **Faxi Taxi** pedicab service is a quick way to get around the centre of the city: find them at taxi stands, or flag one down in the street. Journeys up to 2 km (1 mile) cost €5. One-way journeys more than 2 km cost €10. Services with cab companies **Taxi 31300**, **Taxi 40100** and **Taxi 60160** can be booked by telephone or online.

Driving to Austria

With the exception of Switzerland, all of Austria's neighbours are EU members, meaning there are no border checks. Driving is a pleasant way to reach Vienna as the roads en route are good. The final part of the journey from Bavaria is particularly scenic as you pass through the Alps.

Driving licences issued by any of the European Union member states are valid throughout the EU. If visiting from outside the EU, you may need to apply for an International Driving Permit. Check with your local automobile association before you travel.

Driving in Austria

Austria is a fairly straightforward place to drive. Roads are good and Viennese drivers are generally sensible. Motorways and regional roads are easy to navigate.

Car Rental

Car-hire firms such as **Hertz** and **Sixt Rent-a-Car** can be found at Schwechat Airport. Drivers need to produce their passport, driving licence and a credit card with capacity to cover the excess. Most rental agencies require drivers to be over the age of 21 and to have an international licence.

Parking

Apart from on Sundays, when shops are closed, finding a parking spot in the busy city centre of Vienna can be time consuming. The City of Vienna operates a park-and-pay scheme for all 23 districts from 9am to 10pm during the week. Parking disks are sold at newsagents (*Tabak Trafiken*) and petrol stations. Usually, a maximum stay of two hours is allowed in any space. In some districts, a blue line by the kerb indicates a pay and display scheme. Prices for car parks can vary from €5 per hour to €40 per day.

Rules of the Road

Priority is always given to the right unless a yellow diamond indicates otherwise. Unlike in other EU countries, Austrian stop lights blink rapidly in green before switching to amber. Trams, buses, police cars, fire engines and ambulances all have right of way. Vienna's speed limit is usually 50 km (30 miles) per hour; a speed limit of 30 km (20 miles) per hour is enforced in most residential areas.

Seat belts are compulsory and children under the age of 12 must sit in the back, with babies and toddlers in child seats. In the event of an accident, or if a traffic jam necessitates an abrupt stop, drivers should turn on their hazard lights to warn drivers behind.

The limit for alcohol is 0.5 mg per ml of blood (about 330 ml or half a pint of beer or 1–2 glasses of wine) and is strictly enforced. Spot checks are common and anyone over the limit is likely to face a hefty fine and loss of licence.

Always carry your driving licence as well as car ownership and insurance documents. Every car driving on motorways or expressways is required to display a *vignette* toll sticker, available from all petrol stations, or a digital *vignette*, purchased online. They are valid for 10 days, 2 months or 1 year.

Cycling

Vienna is a great city for cyclists, as long as the main roads and tramlines are avoided. A 7-km (4-mile) cycle path round the Ringstrasse takes you past many historic sights, and there are also paths to the Prater and the Hundertwasserhaus.

Keen cyclists should look out for Radkarte Wien, a booklet illustrating all of Vienna's cycle routes, which is available from bookshops. Bicycles can be rented at some train stations (discounts are given with a train ticket), or from any of the 100 or so **WienMobil** stations located around the city.

Cycling enthusiasts can book tours through **Pedal Power** and **Vienna Explorer**, which offers seats for children as well as e-bikes.

Bicycle Safety

Ride on the right. If you are unsure or unsteady, practise in one of the inner city parks first. Beware of tram tracks; cross them at an angle to avoid getting stuck.

For your own safety, do not walk with your bike in a bike lane or cycle on pavements, on the side of the road, in pedestrian zones or in the dark without lights. Locals may not bother and it isn't compulsory, but wearing a helmet is recommended.

Fiaker

Once the most common form of transport in Vienna, traditional horse-drawn open carriages or *Fiakers*, can still be hired today at Heldenplatz, at Stephansplatz or at Albertinaplatz. There are several companies offering the service, which is now mainly used for special occasions.

Walking

Many of Vienna's major sites are within walking distance of each other, making it an ideal city to cover on foot. The historic Ringstrasse is perfect for a stroll: this pretty boulevard is lined with some of the city's most beautiful buildings, including the Burgtheater.

Those looking for a longer walk can travel just beyond the centre to the beautiful Vienna Woods. Here, you'll find an abundance of scenic hiking paths weaving through vineyards and passing by picturesque towns and villages.

DIRECTORY

TAXI

City of Vienna
w wien.gv.att

Faxi Taxi
w faxi.at

Taxi 31300
w taxi31300.at

Taxi 40100
w taxi40100.at

Taxi 60160
w taxi60160.at

CAR RENTAL

Hertz
w hertz.com

Sixt Rent-a-Car
w sixt.com

CYCLING

Pedal Power
w pedalpower.at

Vienna Explorer
w viennaexplorer.com

WienMobil
w wienerlinien.at

Practical Information

Passports and Visas

For entry requirements, including visas, consult your nearest Austrian embassy or check **Austria Info**. Citizens of the UK, US, Canada, Australia and New Zealand do not need a visa for stays of up to three months but, from late 2023, must apply in advance for the European Travel Information and Authorization System (**ETIAS**). Visitors from other countries may also require an ETIAS, so check before travelling. EU nationals do not need a visa or an ETIAS.

Government Advice

Now more than ever, it is important to consult both your and the Austrian government's advice before travelling. The **UK Foreign, Commonwealth & Development Office (FCDO)**, the **US State Department**, the **Australian Department of Foreign Affairs and Trade** and the **Austrian Foreign Ministry** offer the latest information on security, health and local regulations.

Customs Information

You can find information on the laws relating to goods and currency taken in or out of Austria on the **Austrian Ministry of Finance** website.

Insurance

We recommend that you take out a comprehensive insurance policy covering theft, loss of belongings, medical care, cancellations and delays, and read the small print carefully. If your plans include sporting activities, like skiing, make sure the policy covers this.

Health

Austria has a world-class healthcare system. Emergency medical care is free for all UK and EU citizens, providing they have either a valid EHIC (European Health Insurance Card) or **GHIC** (UK Global Health Insurance Card). Make sure to present this card as soon as possible when receiving emergency medical treatment. You may have to pay upfront and reclaim the money later. For other visitors, payment of hospital and other medical expenses is the patient's responsibility, so it's important to arrange comprehensive medical insurance before travelling.

For information regarding COVID-19 vaccination requirements, consult government advice.

Vienna's many pharmacies (Apotheke) are a very helpful source of information on various medicines and treatments for minor ailments. To locate one, look out for a bright red "A" sign; there is generally one on every major street. Pharmacies run a night and Sunday rota system. Closed pharmacies will display the address of the nearest one open, and the number of the Pharmacy Information Line.

In the event of more serious illnesses and injuries, call the emergency doctor hotline, **Ärztenotdienst**, or make your way to the nearest hospital (Krankenhaus) in the area. Vienna has several private hospitals, clinics and medical centres, but the main facility is Vienna General, the largest hospital in Europe. Most doctors, paramedics and clinic staff speak English.

Dental surgeries are open for both standard and night and weekend services. For out-of-hours help, call the **Emergency Dental Service**.

Unless stated otherwise, tap water in Vienna and its surrounds is safe to drink.

Smoking, Alcohol and Drugs

Austria used to have one of Europe's highest smoking rates. Following most European nations, smoking was finally banned in Austrian bars and restaurants in November 2019.

It is illegal to drive under the influence of alcohol. There are heavy penalties, jail sentences and fines for drug possession depending on the type of narcotic.

ID

There is no requirement for visitors to carry ID, but in the event of a routine check you may be asked to show your passport. If you don't have it with you, the police may escort you to wherever your passport is being kept so that you can show it to them.

Personal Security

Vienna is a relatively safe city to visit, but it's

always a good idea to take precautions when wandering around the city, especially at night. Extra care should be taken against pickpockets, particularly on public transport and in busy tourist areas – especially in and around the Prater. If you have anything stolen, report the crime within 24 hours to the nearest police station and take ID with you. Get a copy of the crime report to make an insurance claim. Contact your embassy if you have your passport stolen, or in the event of a serious crime or accident.

Ambulance, **police** and **fire** services can be called for free. **All emergency services** can also be contacted via the European emergency number.

As a rule, the Viennese are very accepting of all people, regardless of their race, gender or sexuality. Though LGBTQ+ rights in Austria are less progressive than many European countries, homosexuality has been legal since 1971 and in 2009, Austria recognized the right to legally change your gender. If you do feel unsafe, the welcoming **Türkis Rosa Lila Villa**, an LGBTQ+ community centre and café, acts as a safe space.

Travellers with Specific Requirements

Vienna is one of the most accesible cities in Europe. The majority of the transport system is equipped for use by travellers with reduced mobility and hearing and visual impairments. Many of the city's public buses and trams are street-level vehicles with fold-out ramps and a flashing wheelchair symbol to help visitors identify them. Underground stations are equipped with "guiding stripes" to help visually impaired travellers navigate escalators, exits and lifts. A Braille station map of Vienna's underground system can be purchased from the public transport operator Wiener Linien (see p135).

Most major museums are wheelchair accessible and offer audio tours, while many restaurants are wheelchair accessible and offer disabled parking.

The official **Vienna Tourist Board** website has a vast resource that features all accessible attractions, hotels, and restaurants. There are also lists of suppliers that hire out mobility aids and transport companies that provide services for travellers with hearing or visual impairments.

Several companies also offer services to visitors with visual and hearing impairments, including **Bizeps**, the **Austrian Blind Union** and the **Austrian Association for the Hearing Impaired**.

DIRECTORY

PASSPORTS AND VISAS

Austria Info
w austria.info

ETIAS
w etiasvisa.com

GOVERNMENT ADVICE

Australian Department of Foreign Affairs and Trade
w smartraveller.gov.au

Austrian Foreign Ministry
w bmeia.gv.at

UK Foreign, Commonwealth & Development Office (FCDO)
w gov.uk/foreign-travel-advice

US State Department
w travel.state.gov

CUSTOMS INFORMATION

Austrian Ministry of Finance
w bmf.gv.at

HEALTH

Ärztenotdienst
(141

Emergency Dental Service
(01 512 20 78

GHIC
w ghic.org.uk

PERSONAL SECURITY

All Emergency Services
(112

Ambulance
(144

Fire
(122

Police
(133

Türkis Rosa Lila Villa
w dievilla.at

TRAVELLERS WITH SPECIFIC REQUIREMENTS

Austrian Association for the Hearing Impaired
w oeglb.at

Austrian Blind Union
w blindenverband.at

Bizeps
w bizeps.or.at

Vienna Tourist Board
w wien.info

Time Zone

Vienna is in the Central European Time (CET) zone, one hour ahead of Greenwich Mean Time (GMT). Austria switches to daylight saving time (CEST) from the last Sunday in March to the last Sunday in October.

Money

Austria is one of the European countries that uses the euro (€).

Major credit, debit and prepaid currency cards are accepted in most shops and restaurants. Contactless payments are becoming more widely accepted, even on public transport. However, it is always wise to carry some cash, as some smaller businesses won't accept card payments.

Money can be changed at bureaux de change, banks or one of the automated changing machines found across the city. Cash can be withdrawn at banks and ATMs throughout Austria – they are denoted by a sign with the letter "B" in blue and green.

Electrical Appliances

Vienna's standard mains voltage is 230 V. The standard frequency is 50 Hz. Electrical plugs have twin round pins. Devices from North America will need both a frequency adaptor and a voltage converter.

Mobile Phones and Wi-Fi

Visitors travelling to Austria with EU call plans can use their devices abroad without being affected by data roaming charges; instead they are charged the same rates for data, SMS and voice calls as they would pay at home. However, visitors who are staying for extensive periods may find buying an inexpensive Austrian prepaid phone or SIM card worthwhile.

Vienna has more than 400 free Wi-Fi hotspots, including train stations and many hotels. The most popular are in Rathausplatz, the Prater, Stephansplatz, the MuseumsQuartier, the Naschmarkt, and along the Danube Island. The **City of Vienna** website has an interactive map showing the Wi-Fi hotspots. Cafés and restaurants are usually happy to permit the use of their Wi-Fi on the condition that you make a purchase. Wi-Fi is now almost always free in hotels. You can also get online at the tourist information centre on Albertinaplatz.

Postal Services

Austria's postal service, established in 1490, is the oldest standardized postal service in Europe. There are two mailing options from Austria to foreign destinations – priority and economy for Europe and the rest of the world. A standard letter (up to 20g) is automatically posted as priority and will reach the UK in a few days and the US in less than a week.

Stamps are sold at all post offices. Red stripes on a yellow post box indicates that they are emptied on Sundays and public holidays. The city's yellow-fronted post offices are open 8am–noon and 2–6pm Monday–Friday (some stay open during lunch). Suboffices in railway stations are often open 24 hours daily. Find locations and hours on the **Post** website.

Weather

Vienna's biting winds can make winter (late October to March) feel a lot colder than a few degrees below zero. Summer in the city (June to end of August) is usually warm and sunny, but July and August can be sweltering so be sure to book a room with air conditioning if staying in the old city centre.

Opening Hours

Shops are usually open 9am–6:30pm Monday to Friday and 9am–5pm on Saturday; some shopping centres are open until 8pm or 9pm. In this predominantly Catholic country most shops are closed on Sundays, other than in the larger railway stations, at the airport and in the museums.

Most banks are open 8am–12:30pm and 1:30–3pm Monday to Friday (to 5:30pm Friday). In the city centre (1st district) banks don't close for lunch.

Restaurants open daily in the city centre, with those in the outer districts closing for one or two days each week.

Museum opening times vary but most are open 10am–5pm, closing on either Monday or Tuesday. Some of the larger attractions stay open late one evening, often until 9pm.

The COVID-19 pandemic proved that situations can change suddenly. Always check before visiting attractions and hospitality venues for up-to-date hours and booking requirements.

Visitor Information

Multilingual staff offer public transport information, free maps and leaflets about attractions and day trips at tourist offices. Main branches can be found inside the arrivals hall at Vienna International Airport and the Information Point at Central Station as well as at Albertinaplatz/Maysedergasse, with pop-up visitor information booths scattered around the city centre. There's also the **Susi** app, which shows you nearby restaurants, free events, ATMs and pharmacies.

A useful discount card is Wiener Linien's **Vienna City Card**. A "Red" adult pass costs €17, €25 or €29 for 1, 2 or 3 days and provides free entry into over 60 of Vienna's attractions and museums. The pass also entitles travellers to the unlimited use of hop-on-hop-off buses, a free guidebook and an optional public transport pass. Children's passes cost roughly half of an adult pass.

The **Vienna PASS** is only good value if you intend to visit many sights in quite a short period of time.

Vienna Walks & Talks, **Imperial Guide Vienna** and **Wiener Spaziergänge** run fascinating historical walks led by knowledgeable guides that specialize in the arts, music, architecture and social history. They also run many other thematic tours, including culinary and film tours. **Red Bus City Tours** and **Vienna Sightseeing** are veterans of the city's sightseeing routes, with hop-on-hop-off tours on offer.

Visiting Churches

When visiting churches and religious sites, visitors should dress respectfully, avoid raised voices and always keep flash photography to a minimum.

Language

German is Austria's official language but even those with a good grasp may find the Austrian dialects hard to decipher. English is commonly spoken in Vienna, but learning a few niceties in German goes a long way.

Taxes and Refunds

VAT is 20 per cent in Austria. Non-EU residents are entitled to a tax refund subject to certain conditions. In order to do this, you must request a tax receipt and export papers (*Ausfuhrbescheinigung*) when you purchase your goods. When leaving the country, present these papers at Customs, along with the receipt and your ID, to receive your refund.

Accommodation

Vienna has a huge variety of accommodation to suit most budgets, with luxury five-star hotels, family run *pensionen* (B&Bs) and budget hostels.

There's no real low season so it's a good idea to book ahead at any time of year. Prices are inflated at peak times, such as during the summer and Advent.

If on a tight budget, consider staying outside the city centre or pitching up a tent or camper van at one of Vienna's four campsites. Cheap accommodation can also be found in student halls of residence, which are rented out to tourists over the summer. The Vienna Tourist Board *(see p139)* and **Camping Wien** websites offer useful booking resources.

DIRECTORY

MOBILE PHONES AND WI-FI

City of Vienna
w wien.gv.at

POSTAL SERVICES

Post
w post.at

VISITOR INFORMATION

Imperial Guide Viennas
w imperialguide vienna.at

Red Bus City Tours
w redbuscitytours.at

Susi
w susi.at/mobile

Vienna City Card
w viennacitycard.at

Vienna PASS
w viennapass.com

Vienna Sightseeing
w viennasightseeing.at

Vienna Walks & Talks
w viennawalks.com

Wiener Spaziergänge
w wienguide.at

ACCOMMODATION

Camping Wien
w campingwien.at

Places to Stay

PRICE CATEGORIES
For a standard, double room per night (with breakfast if included), taxes and extra charges.

€ under €150   €€ €150–280   €€€ over €280

Luxury Hotels

DO & CO Hotel
MAP N3 ■ Stephansplatz 12 ■ 01 241 88 ■ www.docohotel.com ■ €€€
The DO & CO Hotel is an architectural landmark in the city. The curved glass exterior exudes superior design and advertises the standards of comfort inside. This place has all the amenities of a world-class hotel alongside an impeccable location by the cathedral. The restaurant (see p99) is excellent.

Hotel Bristol
MAP N6 ■ Kärntner Ring 1 ■ 01 515 160 ■ www.bristolvienna.com ■ €€€
One of the top addresses in town, Hotel Bristol is where celebrities and politicians often stay for official or private visits. The 140 rooms offer great views of the Staatsoper opposite. The hotel provides you with all sorts of thoughtful treats, such as umbrellas for rainy days.

Rosewood Vienna
MAP M3 ■ Petersplatz 7 ■ 01 799 98 88 ■ www.rosewoodhotels.com ■ €€€
Housed in the former headquarters of the Erste Group Bank, this luxury hotel comprises 71 stylish guest rooms and 28 suites. There is a spa and fitness centre along with 24-hour in-room dining and a brasserie serving traditional Austrian cuisine. A rooftop bar on the 7th floor offers comfortable seating and stunning city views.

Hotel Sacher
MAP M5 ■ Philharmonikerstrasse 4 ■ 01 514 560 ■ www.sacher.com ■ €€€
Ever since this hotel was founded in 1876 it has been a Viennese institution, with guests ranging from emperors and diplomats to artists. At the café next door, writers such as Arthur Schnitzler used to enjoy the famous Sachertorte with a coffee. The hotel still ranks among Vienna's most luxurious. All rooms are individually furnished.

Imperial
MAP N6 ■ Kärntner Ring 16 ■ 01 501 100 ■ www.imperialvienna.com ■ €€€
This grand hotel opened in 1873 and soon turned into a meeting place for Austro-Hungarian nobility. It still retains its regal charm. Delights from the hotel's confectioners include the Imperialtorte, created in honour of Emperor Franz Joseph I at the hotel's opening.

Marriott Vienna
MAP P5 ■ Parkring 12a ■ 01 515 180 ■ www.viennamarriott.at ■ €€€
The Marriott is within walking distance of all the famous landmarks. It has an indoor swimming pool and a health club where guests can relax after a hard day's sightseeing.

Palais Coburg Hotel Residenz
MAP P4 ■ Coburgbastei 4 ■ 01 518 180 ■ www.palais-coburg.com ■ €€€
This luxurious hotel is housed in a 19th-century building. There are health and beauty facilities, and the Coburg spa on the top floor offers good views.

The Ritz – Carlton
MAP E5 ■ Schubertring 5–7 ■ 01 311 88 ■ www.ritzcarlton.com/vienna ■ €€€
Located on the historic Ringstrasse, close to the Stadtpark, this hotel offers spacious rooms with modern design, a state-of-the-art fitness centre, an indoor pool and spa facilities.

Vienna Intercontinental
MAP Q6 ■ Johannesgasse 28 ■ 01 711 220 ■ www.intercontinental.com/Vienna ■ €€€
This luxurious five-star modern hotel is located conveniently opposite the Stadtpark and not far from the Konzerthaus. It offers 453 plush rooms.

Hotels in Great Locations

Das Opernring
MAP M5 ■ Opernring 11 ■ 01 587 55 180 ■ www.opernring.at ■ €
Built in the Historicist style of the Ringstrasse, this hotel is opposite the Staatsoper. The balconies overlook the tree-lined

Ring and offer great views along the boulevard. There is no air-conditioning here.

Hotel Park-Villa

Hasenauerstrasse 12 ▪ Bus 40A ▪ 01 367 57 00 ▪ www.parkvilla.at ▪ €
Situated in the elegant Döbling neighbourhood, this magnificent villa turned hotel was once used by well-off Viennese to spend their summers. Most rooms have balconies and the terrace leads into the garden.

Seminarhotel Springer Schlössl

Tivoligasse 73 ▪ Bus 9A ▪ 01 814 20 49 ▪ www.springer-schloessl.at ▪ €
Housed in a castle built in 1887 and set in a large park near the famous Schloss Schönbrunn, this hotel has good facilities for business travellers.

Grand Hotel Wien

MAP N6 ▪ Kärntner Ring 9 ▪ 01 515 800 ▪ www.grandhotelwien.com ▪ €€
Opened in 1870, the Grand Hotel Wien is housed in an elegant mansion located along the Ringstrasse and has an early 20th-century feel. It has 250 rooms and suites, which are decorated in Art Nouveau style.

Hilton Vienna Danube Waterfront

Handelskai 269 ▪ Train Stadion; U-Bahn 2 ▪ 01 72 777 ▪ www3.hilton.com ▪ €€
Located close to the football stadium, this luxury accommodation offers first-rate amenities. It has an outdoor pool on the riverbank, and advertises itself as "Austria's leading business hotel".

Hotel Am Stephansplatz

MAP N3 ▪ Stephansplatz 9 ▪ 01 534 050 ▪ www.hotelamstephansplatz.at ▪ €€
Situated in the heart of Vienna, this hotel has first-class amenities. Many rooms have a view of the cathedral.

Hotel Regina

MAP C3 ▪ Rooseveltplatz 15 ▪ 01 404 460 ▪ www.kremslehnerhotels.at ▪ €€
The Hotel Regina has a terrific view of the Neo-Gothic Votivkirche, with rooms overlooking the church's roof and its high stone towers. Besides the popular hotel café, the stylish Roth restaurant can be found on the ground floor. There is no air-conditioning.

Hotel Schloss Wilhelminenberg

Savoyenstrasse 2 ▪ Bus 146B ▪ 01 485 85 03 ▪ www.austria-trend.at ▪ €€
Count Lacy, an Austrian aristocrat, had this palace built between 1781 and 1784 on his vast hunting grounds on top of the Wilhelminen mountain. The hotel offers great views of Vienna and is very well located – it only takes about 30 minutes to get here from the city centre. The hotel has no air-conditioning.

The Ring

MAP N6 ▪ Kärntner Ring 8 ▪ 01 22 1220 ▪ www.theringhotel.com ▪ €€€
Just a stone's throw away from the Staatsoper and main shopping district, this lovely boutique hotel is located directly on the Ring. Rooms here are sumptuously decorated and there is also a fitness room, steam bath, sauna and spa on site.

Sans Souci

MAP E1 ▪ Burggasse 2 ▪ 01 522 25 20 ▪ www.sanssouci-wien.com ▪ €€€
Steps away from the MuseumsQuartier, this deluxe hotel is right in the centre of Vienna's hippest area. Facilities include a swimming pool and spa, and all rooms are air-conditioned. Sans Souci is a superb blend of traditional architecture and modern comfort.

Historic Hotels

Hotel Rathauspark

MAP J2 ▪ Rathausstrasse 17 ▪ 01 404 12 ▪ www.austria-trend.at ▪ €
This hotel was the home of the Austrian writer Stefan Zweig and you can still experience the atmosphere of imperial Vienna here. It is close to the Town Hall and the iconic Café Central. No air-conditioning.

Mercure Grand Hotel Biedermeier Wien

MAP R4 ▪ Landstrasser Hauptstrasse 28 ▪ 01 716 710 ▪ www.all.accor.com ▪ €
Housed in an early 19th-century building in a peaceful location, this hotel is within walking distance of major sights including the Belvedere, the Ring as well as the Stephansdom. The lovely Biedermeier house has a quiet inner courtyard and a conservatory restaurant. Pets are allowed for an additional €10.

Ambassador

MAP N4 ■ Neuer Markt 5/Kärntner Strasse 22 ■ 01 961 610 ■ www. ambassador.at ■ €€

Baroque architect Fischer von Erlach constructed this house in the late 17th century and in 1898 it became a hotel. Famous guests have included the writer Mark Twain and actress Marlene Dietrich. It's still one of Vienna's most charming hotels.

Hotel König von Ungarn

MAP N3 ■ Schulerstrasse 10 ■ 01 515 840 ■ www. kvu.at ■ €€

The "King of Hungary" hotel is housed in a historic building that dates back to the 1600s. During the Austro-Hungarian monarchy, Hungarian aristocrats rented apartments here. Many of their names are inscribed in the hotel's guest book.

Hotel Mailbergerhof

MAP N5 ■ Annagasse 7 ■ 01 512 06 41 ■ www. mailbergerhof.at ■ €€

The fascinating history of this house dates from the 14th century, although the original Gothic building was converted into a small Baroque palace with stables and its own chapel. The 40 rooms here are cosy, well-appointed and non-smoking.

Hotel Orient

MAP M2 ■ Tiefer Graben 30–32 ■ 01 533 72 07 ■ www.hotelorient.at ■ €€

Built in 1896, the Hotel Orient is on an old riverbank that linked the city with the Danube. Here, trading ships unloaded cargo from the Orient years ago. The hotel has an opulent *fin-de-siècle* interior, but note that many of the rooms are rented by the hour. No air-conditioning.

Parkhotel Schönbrunn

Hietzinger Hauptstrasse 10–14 ■ Tram 58 ■ 01 878 040 ■ www.austria-trend.at ■ €€

Emperor Franz Joseph I had this stately mansion built in 1907 near Schloss Schönbrunn to accommodate his guests. The hotel offers modern amenities but retains a hint of the imperial splendour of bygone times. There is no air-conditioning.

Pertschy Palais Hotel

MAP M3 ■ Habsburgergasse 5 ■ 01 534 490 ■ www. pertschy.com ■ €€

Aristocrat Maximilian von Cavriani had a Baroque palace built here in 1734. The lovely building is now a privately run B&B with an inner courtyard and 55 rooms equipped with modern amenities.

Schlosshotel Römischer Kaiser

MAP N5 ■ Annagasse 16 ■ 01 512 77 510 ■ www. gshotels.de/roemischer kaiser ■ €€

This hotel is housed in a Baroque palace dating from 1684 in a side street off Kärntner Strasse. The foyer and some rooms still have historic features.

Wandl

MAP M3 ■ Petersplatz 9 ■ 01 534 550 ■ www. hotel-wandl.com ■ €€

Set in an 18th-century house, this family-run hotel has cosy rooms but no air-conditioning.

Family-Friendly Hotels

Art Hotel

Brandmayergasse 9 ■ 01 544 51 08 ■ www. thearthotelvienna.at ■ €

As the name suggests, this hotel features a lot of art. Located near the colourful street market Naschmarkt, it is just 20 minutes away by bus from Stephansdom. It offers Inexpensive large family rooms with kitchens, and underground parking but no air-conditioning.

Hotel Josefshof Am Rathaus

MAP D2 ■ Josefsgasse 4–6 ■ 01 404 190 ■ www. josefshof.com ■ €

This hotel is situated on a quiet road in a central location. Breakfast is served until noon. The Josefshof is a good choice for families as one child under the age of 16 can stay for free in a room with both parents.

Stadthotel Henriette

MAP R1 ■ Praterstrasse 44–6 ■ 01 214 84 04 ■ www.hotelhenriette.at ■ €€

Centrally situated halfway between Stephansdom and the Prater amusement park, this family-run hotel offers modern, hypoallergenic rooms with balconies and spacious suites. Great breakfasts with vegetarian and vegan options.

Erzherzog Rainer

MAP G4 ■ Wiedner Hauptstrasse 27–29 ■ 01 221 11 ■ www.hotel erzhograiner.wien ■ €€

A short walk from the Belvedere Palace, this large, old-fashioned hotel is one of the five Vienna Schick family hotels. Children are warmly welcomed and babysitting is available. All rooms are non-smoking, and there is no air conditioning.

The Harmonie
MAP B3 ■ Harmoniegasse 5–7 ■ 01 317 66 04 ■ www.harmonie-vienna.at ■ €€
A stylish and comfortable boutique hotel, serving free tea and cakes in the lounge and library. Rooms are decorated with paintings by artist Luis Casanova Sorolla.

Hotel am Parkring
MAP Q4 ■ Parkring 12 ■ 01 514 800 ■ www.hotelamparkring.wien ■ €€
Located on the elegant Ringstrasse, the 58-room Hotel am Parkring offers a splendid view of the tree-lined avenue from the 13th floor. It is a great choice for families. For its younger guests, plenty of books and toys are available and babysitters can be easily organized. The restaurant also offers children's menus.

Hotel Anatol
MAP G1 ■ Webgasse 26 ■ 01 599 96 ■ www.austria-trend.at/hotel-anatol ■ €€
Around the corner from Mariahilfer Strasse, Hotel Anatol has large family rooms with child-friendly facilties. Toys are available and a babysitter can be arranged.

Hotel City Central
MAP Q1 ■ Taborstrasse 8 ■ 01 211 500 ■ www.hotelcitycentral.wien ■ €€
Located on the edge of the city centre, this is an ideal point from which to discover the city. This four-star hotel was built at the beginning of the 20th century. Children under six stay free; those between six and twelve stay for half price.

Hotel Lassalle
Engerthstrasse 173–5 ■ U-Bahn U1 ■ 01 213 150 ■ www.austria-trend.at ■ €€
This modern hotel is ideally situated for families, as the Danube island with all its lawns and cycling paths is close by. There are family rooms, a games room and playroom for children with toys and books. You can arrange babysitters on request at reception. No air-conditioning.

Hotel Stefanie
MAP Q1 ■ Taborstrasse 12 ■ 01 211 500 ■ www.hotelstefanie.wien ■ €€
Named after the wife of Crown Prince Rudolph, Hotel Stefanie is located just beyond the Danube canal and only a few minutes' walk from the city centre. Toys and special menus for kids are available, as well as reliable babysitting services. Of the hotel's 131 guest rooms, some are extra-large accommodation meant for families.

Starlight Suite Hotel Wien am Heumarkt
MAP E6 ■ Am Heumarkt 15 ■ 01 710 78 08 ■ www.starlighthotels.com ■ €€
Situated right next to the Stadtpark, this modern hotel offers large, well-appointed suites, as well as regular bedrooms. Guests can avail a free breakfast here. Children under the age of 12 stay free of charge.

Medium-Priced Hotels

Am Schottenpoint
MAP B3 ■ Währinger Strasse 22 ■ 01 310 87 87 ■ www.schottenpoint.at ■ €
This small hotel is a friendly place with 17 non-air-conditioned rooms. It's only a short walk away from the Ring and only a few minutes from the tram, bus and underground services into the centre. A breakfast buffet is included in the price of the room.

Carlton Opera
MAP F3 ■ Schikanedergasse 4 ■ 01 587 53 02 ■ www.carlton.at ■ €
Located on the edge of the city centre, the Carlton Opera is an ideal starting point for exploring the city. Karlskirche is just around the corner and the MuseumsQuartier is also nearby. All its 57 rooms have tea- and coffee-making facilities. Apartments with family rooms and a kitchen are also available.

Cryston
MAP H1 ■ Gaudenzdorfer Gürtel 63 ■ 01 813 56 82 ■ www.hotel-cryston.hotelsinvienna.org ■ €
The cosy, friendly rooms of the Hotel Cryston make up for its location on a busy road. The modern bedrooms are fitted with satellite TV, direct-dial phones, a safe, and hairdryers in the en-suite bathrooms, but there is no air-conditioning.

For a key to hotel price categories see p142

Hotel Austria
MAP P2 ▪ Fleischmarkt 20 ▪ 01 515 23 ▪ www.hotelaustria-wien.at ▪ €
The Hotel Austria, located in a cul-de-sac, offers peace and quiet even though it is in the middle of Vienna. It has 42 rooms and four apartments, and there is also the cheaper option of picking a room without an en-suite.

Hotel Prinz Eugen
MAP H5 ▪ Wiedner Gürtel 14 ▪ 01 505 17 41 ▪ www.novum-hotels.com/hotel-prinz-eugen-wien ▪ €
This standard city hotel is situated in the embassy district, close to the Belvedere. The decor is an eclectic mix – some of the rooms are traditional and some are modern.

Novum Hotel Congress Wien
MAP H5 ▪ Wiedner Gürtel 34 ▪ 01 505 55 06 ▪ www.novum-hotels.de ▪ €
Situated just across from the former Südbahnhof and set very close to the Belvedere on a fairly busy road, this is a modern three-star hotel. All 75 rooms and two apartments are good value, have satellite television and internet access.

Ruby Marie
Kaiserstrasse 2–4 ▪ 01 205 63 97 00 ▪ www.ruby-hotels.com ▪ €
Near the Westbahnhof, the Ruby Marie hotel is trendy and offers amazing value for money. The rooftop bar area is large, and has great views. Both bikes and electric guitars are available for hire here and there is also a yoga

space and a library, as well as a 25-seat cinema for guests.

Alma Boutique-Hotel
MAP P2 ▪ Hafnersteig 7 ▪ 01 533 29 61 ▪ www.hotel-alma.com ▪ €€
The once modest Pension Christina has undergone a complete makeover and now features stylish decor. The hotel's 26 rooms have a range of amenities, such as whirlpool baths in a few rooms. Located in the heart of Vienna, it is within walking distance of the famous sights. Visitors can also enjoy excellent views from the terrace.

Daniel Wien
MAP H6 ▪ Landstrasser Gürtel 5 ▪ 01 901 310 ▪ www.hoteldaniel.com/vienna ▪ €€
This smart, minimalist hotel in the Belvedere quarter has its own bakery on site. Guests can hire iPads and Vespa scooters. You can even sleep in a luxury 1952 aluminium Airstream trailer in the garden.

Hotel de France
MAP L1 ▪ Schottenring 3 ▪ 01 313 680 ▪ www.hoteldefrance.at ▪ €€
Built in 1872, this hotel retains the elegant style of this era, which is now combined with modern comforts. Facilities at the hotel include conference and banqueting halls, and three restaurants.

Kugel
MAP E2 ▪ Siebensterngasse 43 ▪ 01 523 33 55 ▪ Closed 9 Jan–29 Feb ▪ www.hotelkugel.at ▪ €€
Hotel Kugel, located next to the Spittelberg area,

has been in operation since 1899. It offers free Wi-Fi, a relaxed atmosphere and tasteful rooms, some with four-poster beds. There is no air-conditioning.

Marc Aurel
MAP N2 ▪ Marc-Aurel-Strasse 8 ▪ 01 533 36 400 ▪ www.hotel-marcaurel.com ▪ €€
Located only minutes away from Stephansdom, this hotel in the heart of Vienna has 18 rooms, some of them suitable for people with specific needs. There are also two large rooms with a kitchenette.

Rathaus Wine & Design
MAP D2 ▪ Lange Gasse 13 ▪ 01 400 11 22 ▪ www.hotel-rathaus-wien.at ▪ €€
Everything revolves around wine at this designer hotel close to the city centre. Each of the rooms is dedicated to a top Austrian wine-grower, there is a wine and cheese breakfast, and there are wine cosmetics in the rooms.

Renaissance Wien Hotel
Linke Wienzeile/Ullmanstrasse 71 ▪ U-Bahn U4 ▪ 01 891 020 ▪ www.renaissance wien.at ▪ €€
Part of the Marriott chain, this modern hotel with luxurious furnishings is situated near Schloss Schönbrunn and is just ten minutes on the underground from the city centre sights. Alongside other facilities, there is an indoor rooftop pool.

Budget Hotels

Ani
**Kinderspitalgasse 1
■ U-Bahn U6 ■ 01 405
65 53 ■ www.pension-ani.
hotelsinvienna.org ■ €**
Pension Ani is a simple
B&B in an old building
with rooms in various
sizes, but there is no air-
conditioning and some
toilets are shared. It is
close to the underground
U6 and trams.

Bleckmann
**MAP C3 ■ Währinger
Strasse 15 ■ 01 408 08
99 ■ www.hotel
bleckmann.at ■ €**
This cosy family-run hotel
is set in the Schottenring
and Alsergrund quarter,
where Sigmund Freud,
Franz Schubert and many
other famous Viennese
personalities lived. The
rooms are simple and
nicely furnished, though
not air-conditioned, and
there is a breakfast buffet.

Boltzmann
**MAP B2 ■ Boltzmann-
gasse 8 ■ 01 354 500
■ www.hotelboltzmann.at
■ €**
Set near the Gartenpalais
Liechtenstein, this child-
friendly hotel is in an ideal
location for exploring
Vienna on foot and for
enjoying the vibrant 9th
district. The courtyard
garden, underground
parking and reasonable
room rates mean that
early booking is essential.

Drei Kronen
Wien City
**MAP F4 ■ Schleifmühl-
gasse 25 ■ 01 587 32 89
■ www.hotel3kronen.at
■ €**
Although its building is
more than 100 years old,

this hotel has modern
rooms all equipped with
a TV and internet access.
It is located in a lively
neighbourhood, near the
Secession Building and
Karlskirche, with many
restaurants, pubs and
bars nearby. There's also
a good breakfast buffet.
No air-conditioning.

Haydn
**MAP F2 ■ Mariahilfer
Strasse 57–9 ■ 01 587
44 140 ■ www.haydn-
hotel.at ■ €**
This three-star hotel is
set on one of Vienna's
main shopping streets,
Mariahilfer Strasse, and
has an underground
station right by its front
door. The rooms are quiet
and are equipped with a
telephone, cable TV and
a minibar. The hotel also
has other options such as
apartments with kitchen
facilities and suites.

Kaffeemühle
**Kaiserstrasse 45 ■ 01
523 86 88 ■ www.kaffee
muhle.com ■ €**
Acquired by the Novum
hotel chain, the "Coffee
Mill" offers stylish urban
design. Its location in the
hip Neubau area of the
city enables convenient
access to public transport.
Clean and inexpensive,
it is very high in demand,
so early booking is highly
advised. There is no
air-conditioning.

Kolping Wien Zentral
**MAP F3 ■ Stiegengasse
12/Corner Gumpendorfer-
strasse 39 ■ 01 587 56
310 ■ www.kolping-wien-
zentral.at ■ €**
Located in a small side
street not far from the
MuseumsQuartier, most
of the modern rooms in

this guest house are very
quiet. There's a range
of non-air-conditioned
rooms and visitors can
choose between various
sizes and standards of
accommodation. A break
fast buffet is included in
the price of the room.

Nossek
**MAP M3 ■ Graben 17
■ 01 533 70 41 11 ■ www.
pension-nossek.at ■ €**
This B&B is located in the
pedestrian zone of Graben,
right in the middle of the
bustling city centre. Its 26
rooms are cosy and fitted
with all mod cons. There
is also a TV room, and
families are welcome.

Vienna Westend
City Hostel
**Fügergasse 3 ■ U-Bahn
U3, U6 ■ 01 597 67 29
■ No credit cards ■ www.
viennahostel.at ■ €**
This hostel close to the
Westbahnhof railway
station has simple non-air-
conditioned rooms, each
with toilet and shower
facilities. The building has
a spiral staircase but there
is also a lift and a small
garden. Facilities include
a bike-locker room and a
communal TV room.

magdas Hotel
**■ MAP R5 ■ Ungargasse
38 ■ 01 720 02 88 ■ www.
magdas-hotel.at ■ €**
Founded as a social
enterprise, this hotel is
near the Belvedere. There
are 85 rooms including a
family suite and two fully
wheelchair-accessible
rooms all featuring
upcycled furniture and
air-conditioning. There is
also a restaurant with an
outside eating area serving
meals made from regional
and organic produce.

For a key to hotel price categories see p142

General Index

Acknowledgments

This edition updated by

Contributor Melanie Nicholson-Hartzell
Senior Editor Alison McGill
Senior Art Editor Stuti Tiwari
Project Editors Dipika Dasgupta, Lucy Sara-Kelly
Assistant Art Editor Divyanshi Shreyaskar
Assistant Editors Ilina Choudhary, Tavleen Kaur
Picture Research Administrator Vagisha Pushp
Publishing Assistant Halima Mohammed
Picture Research Manager Taiyaba Khatoon
Jacket Designer Jordan Lambley
Cartographer Ashif
Cartography Manager Suresh Kumar
Senior DTP Designer Tanveer Zaidi
Senior Production Editor Jason Little
Production Controller Kariss Ainsworth
Deputy Managing Editor Beverly Smart
Managing Editors Shikha Kulkarni, Hollie Teague
Managing Art Editor Sarah Snelling
Senior Managing Art Editor Priyanka Thakur
Art Director Maxine Pedliham
Publishing Director Georgina Dee

DK would like to thank the following for
their contribution to the previous editions:
Clive Streeter, Kathryn Glendenning, Michael
Leidig, Helen Peters, Peter Wilson, Sarah
Woods, Irene Zoech

The publisher would like to thank the following
for their kind permission to reproduce their
photographs:

Key: a-above; b-below/bottom; c-centre; f-far;
l-left; r-right; t-top

123RF.com: ginasanders 106cla, Kabvisio 74tr;
kisamarkiza 91t, Pavel Lipskiy 83b, 102b, Meinzahn
122b, Alexandr Mychko 75bl, Roman Plesky 100ca,
Anna Pustynnikova 75tr, radub85 107b, 117cla,
tasfoto 81br, Yaroslav Yatsyk 126cla, zechal 116ca.

Alamy Stock Photo: Luise Berg-Ehlers 76tr;
blickwinkel / Samot 105cl; Svetlana Dingarac
87tr; Robert Dziewulski 112-3; edpics 67cl;
Manfred Gottschalk 40clb; Granger Historical
Picture Archive 48ca; Hackenberg-Photo-Cologne
62b, 80tl, 80br, 99tr, 116b; Hemis.fr / Ludovic
Maisant 29tl; imageBROKER / Egon Bömsch
32cla; John Kellerman 16-7c, 26-7, 65tr;
Brian_Kinney 10cla; Art Kowalsky 1, 2tl, 3tr, 8-9,
132-3; LOOK Die Bildagentur der Fotografen
GmbH / Ingolf Pompe 105br; Stefano Politi
Markovina 4cl; mauritius images GmbH / Volker
Preusser 81cla; McPhoto / Bilderbox 14cl; David
Noton 10clb; Prisma by Dukas Presseagentur
GmbH 43ca; robertharding / Michael Runkel 11br;
Romas_ph 3tl, 88-9; Sagaphoto.com / Stephane
Gautier 73tr; Riccardo Sala 29cr; Maurice Savage
18cra; travelimages 4cra; volkerpreusser 107cb;
Ernst Wrba 45br.

© Albertina, Vienna: 7cla, 91crb.

Architekturzentrum Wien: Lisa Rastl 35cra.

AWL Images: Neil Farrin 10bl; Stefano Politi
Markovina 11clb.

B&F Wien: Manfred Seidl 67tl.

Belvedere, Vienna: 28bl, 31bl.

Burgtheater: 93cl.

Café Do-An: 119cla.

Café Museum: 118ca.

Circus and Clown Museum: 57tr.

Das Mo öbel: 110b.

Das Triest - Bistro Porto: Steve Herud 125b.

© Palais Daun-Kinsky, Wien: Herbert
Lehmann 53cl.

Der Dritte Mann Tour: Felicitas Matern 62tl.

Dorotheum: R. R. Rumpler 96tl.

Dreamstime.com: Abxyz 4crb; Rostislav Ageev
7tr; Alexirina27000 17tl; David Bailey 54cl, 64tr;
Maksim Budnikov 101bc; Nikolay Bychkov 36br;
Chaoss 6bl, 73cl; Dafrei 52tl; Dagobert1620 130b;
Digitalpress 51bl; Mindauga Dulinska 12cl, 41tl;
Dziewul 40cr, 128tr; Darius Dzinnik 75cl;
Empire331 85cl; Iakov Filimonov 87cla; Denitsa
Glavinova 44cl; Özgür Güvenç 55t; Fritz Hiersche
129cla; Kisamarkiza 44b, 86tl; Derii Larisa 74bl;
Erik Lattwein 79crb; Pavel Lipskiy 38br, 59b; Fabio
Lotti 4clb; Lucasarts 128-9b; Marcin Łukaszewicz
11tl; Magition 32br; Meinzahn 4t, 63tr, 70–1, 104b;
Mikolaj64 84tl; minnystock 17cr; Mircea Hotea
76tr; Anna Nakonechna 19tr; Olgalngs 15crb;
Lefteris Papaulakis 12-3; Pavel068 11cla; Bojan
Pavlukovic 90cla; Photoblueice 53br; Roman
Plesky 50t; Radub85 56br, 58clb; Romasph 115br;
Scanrail 28-9c; Jozef Sedmak 101t, 120cla;
Sjankauskas 60bc; Nikolai Sorokin 18tl; Svetlana195
4b, 54bc, 61kr; TasFoto 16cla, 41crb, 85tr, 102tl;
Tomas1111 36cl, 92cl, 94bl; Vitalyedush 12clb;
Vvoevale 92bc; Bettina Wagner 4cla; Xalanx 13tr;
Minyun Zhou 33br.

EssDur Restaurant im Konzerthaus: 79tl.

Fabios: 99clb.

Getty Images: adoc-photos 19bl; AFP / Patrick
Domingo 6tr; / Joe Klamar 83tr; / Dieter Nagl 84b;
Getty Images Europe / Manfred Schmid 72bl;
Gonzalo Azumendi 115tl; De Agostini Picture
Library 60clb; DEA / A. Dagli Orti 45clb, 49tr, 61cl;
/ E. Lessing 31tr; / G. Dagli Orti 60tr; Pascal
Deloche 2tr, 46–7, 121t; Godong 77cla; Jorg
Greuel 121b; Hulton Deutsch 49cl; Hulton Fine
Art Collection 48b; Imagno 15cla, 21b, 30tr, 37tl;
Herbert Neubauer 72t; Sylvain Sonnet 33tl; UIG /
JTB Photo 121tr; Ullstein Bild 15clb, / Karin
Nussbaumer 70crb.

Haus der Musik: Rudi Froese 57cl.

ImPulsTanz: Karolina Miernik 86cr.

iStockphoto.com: alessandro0770 37bl;
VvoeVale 59tl.

© KHM-Museumsverband: 22cra, 22cl, 22bl,
23tl, 23cra, 24cl, 24bl, 25tr, 25c, 25b.

Leopold Museum, Vienna: Self, Portrait with
Chinese Lantern Plant (1912) Egon Schiele, Oil,
opaque colour on wood, 32,2 × 39,8 cm 11cra;
WienTourismus / Peter Rigaud 35tl.

Marionettentheater Schloss Schönbrunn:
Roman Gerhardt 68t.

Meinl am Graben: Herbert Lehmann 95bc.

Meixner's Gastwirtschaft: 131cra.

MuseumsQuartier E+B GesmbH: Hertha
Hurnaus 108–9.

Österreichische Akademie der Wissenschaften:
Klaus Pichler 94tr.

© Palais Ferstel, Vienna: Christian Husar 76–7b;
Herbert Lehmann 98b; Michael Rzepa 52br.

Salm Bräu: Mario Kranabetter 124tl.

Copyright Schloss Schönbrunn Kultur- und Betriebsges.m.b.H.: 42bl, 43bl; Bildagentur Zolles KG / Christian Hofer 42c; Knaack 17br; Julius Silver 64–5b.

Shutterstock.com: Erich Karnberger 108tc, Kiev. Victor 34–5c.

Sigmund Freud Museum: Oliver Ottenschlaeger 103cla.

Sky Bar: 97b.

Spanish Riding School: ASAblanca.com / Rene é van Bakel 20t, 20c; Mathias Lauringer 20bl.

Steffl: Michael Sazel 82t.

Steirereck im Stadtpark: © pierer.net 78b.

SuperStock: 14br, 86–7; age fotostock / Carlos S. Pereyra 41bl; F1 ONLINE 51cra; imageBROKER 77tr.

Technisches Museum Wien: 68clb; Peter Sedlaczek 56t.

Tunnel: 111cla.

Vienna Secession: Jorit Aust 39tl; Oliver Ottenschlaeger 38–9; Wolfgang Thaler 11cr, 39br.

© www.lupispuma.com / Volkstheater: 70tl, 107tr.

Wein & Co Bar: 118br.

Wien Museum: Hertha Hurnaus 123tl, 127br; Lisa Rastl 66b.

Xocolat: 95cl.

Zoom Kindermuseum: Alexandra Eizinger 69cra; J. J. Kucek 34bl.

Cover

Front and spine: **Alamy Stock Photo:** Art Kowalsky.

Back: **Dreamstime.com:** Mistervlad cla, Rosshelen crb, Sborisov tr, Zwawol tl; **Alamy Stock Photo:** Art Kowalsky b.

Pull Out Map Cover

Alamy Stock Photo: Art Kowalsky.

All other images © Dorling Kindersley
For further information see:
www.dkimages.com

Illustrator: Chris Orr & Associates chrisorr.com.

Penguin
Random
House

First edition 2003

Published in Great Britain by
Dorling Kindersley Limited
DK, One Embassy Gardens, 8 Viaduct Gardens, London SW11 7BW, UK

The authorised representative in the EEA is Dorling Kindersley Verlag GmbH. Arnulfstr. 124, 80636 Munich, Germany

Published in the United States by
DK Publishing, 1745 Broadway, 20th Floor, New York, NY 10019, USA

Copyright © 2003, 2023
Dorling Kindersley Limited
A Penguin Random House Company

23 24 25 26 10 9 8 7 6 5 4 3 2 1

A CIP catalogue record is available
from the British Library.

A catalogue record for this book is available
from the Library of Congress.

ISSN 1479-344X
ISBN 978-0-2416-1875-2

Printed and bound in Malaysia

www.dk.com

As a guide to abbreviations in visitor information blocks: **Adm** = admission charge; **D** = dinner; **L** = Lunch.

MIX
Paper | Supporting
responsible forestry
FSC™ C018179

This book was made with Forest Stewardship Council™ certified paper – one small step in DK's commitment to a sustainable future.
**For more information go to
www.dk.com/our-green-pledge**

Phrase Book

In an Emergency

Where is the telephone?	Wo ist das Telefon?	voh ist duss tel-e-fone?
Help!	Hilfe!	hilf-uh
Please call a doctor	Bitte rufen Sie einen Arzt	bitt-uh roof'n zee ine-en artst
Please call the police	Bitte rufen Sie die Polizei	bitt-uh roof'n zee dee poli-tsy
Please call the fire brigade	Bitte rufen Sie die Feuerwehr	bitt-uh roof'n zee dee foyer-vayr
Stop!	Halt!	hult

Communication Essentials

Yes	Ja	yah
No	Nein	nine
Please	Bitte	bitt-uh
Thank you	Danke	dunk-uh
Excuse me	Verzeihung	fair-tsy-hoong
Hello (good day)	Guten Tag	goot-en tahk
Goodbye	Auf Wiedersehen	owf-veed-er-zay-ern
Good evening	Guten Abend	goot'n ahb'nt
Good night	Gute Nacht	goot-uh nukht
Why?	Warum?	var-room
Where?	Wo?	voh
When?	Wann?	vunn
today	heute	hoyt-uh
tomorrow	morgen	morg'n
month	Monat	mohn-aht
night	Nacht	nukht
afternoon	Nachmittag	nahkh-mit-tahk
morning	Morgen	morg'n
year	Jahr	yar
there	dort	dort
here	hier	hear
week	Woche	vokh-uh
yesterday	gestern	gest'n
evening	Abend	ahb'nt

Useful Phrases

How are you?	Wie geht's?	vee gayts
Fine, thanks	Danke, es geht mir gut	dunk-uh, es gayt meer goot
Where is/are?	Wo ist/sind...?	voh ist/sind
How far is it to...?	Wie weit ist es...?	vee vite ist ess
Do you speak English?	Sprechen Sie Englisch?	shpresh'n zee eng-glish
I don't understand	Ich verstehe nicht	ish fair-shtay-uh nisht
Please speak more slowly	Bitte, sprechen Sie langsamer	bitte shpresh'n zee lang-zammer

Useful Words

large	gross	grohss
small	klein	kline
hot	heiss	hyce
cold	kalt	kult
good	gut	goot
bad	böse/schlecht	burss-uh/shlesht
open	geöffnet	g'urff-nett
closed	geschlossen	g'shloss'n
left	links	links
right	rechts	reshts

Making a Telephone Call

I would like to make a phone call	Ich möchte telefonieren	ish mer-shtuh tel-e-fon-eer'n
I'll try again later	Ich versuche noch ein mal später	ish fair-zookh-uh r nokh ine-mull shpay-te
Can I leave a message?	Kann ich eine Nachricht hinterlassen?	kan ish ine-uh nakh-risht hint-er-lahss-en
telephone card	Telefonkarte	tel-e-fohn-kart-uh
mobile phone	Mobiltelfon	mobeel tel-e-fone
engaged (busy)	besetzt	b'zetst
wrong number	Falsche Verbindung	falsh-uh fair-bin-doong

Sightseeing

entrance ticket	Eintrittskarte	ine-tritz-kart-uh
cemetery	Friedhof	freed-hofe
train station	Bahnhof	barn-hofe
gallery	Galerie	gall-er-ee
information	Auskunft	owss-koonft
church	Kirche	keersh-uh
garden	Garten	gart'n
palace/castle	Palast/Schloss	pallast/shloss
place (square)	Platz	plats
bus stop	Haltestelle	hal-te-shtel-uh
national holiday	Nationalfeiertag	nats-yon-ahl-fire-tahk
theatre	Theater	tay-aht-er
free admission	Eintritt frei	ine-tritt fry

Shopping

Do you have...?	Gibt es...?	geept ess
How much does it cost?	Was kostet das?	voss kost't duss
When do you open/close?	Wann öffnen Sie/ schliessen Sie?	vunn off'n zee shlees'n zee
this	das	duss
expensive	teuer	toy-er
cheap	preiswert	price-vurt
size	Grösse	gruhs-uh
number	Nummer	noom-er
colour	Farbe	farb-uh
brown	braun	brown
black	schwarz	shvarts
red	rot	roht
blue	blau	blau
green	grün	groon
yellow	gelb	gelp

Types of Shop

antiques shop	Antiquariat	antik-var-yat
chemist (pharmacy)	Apotheke/ Drogerie	appo-tay-kuh/ droog-er-ree
bank	Bank	bunk
market	Markt	markt
travel agency	Reisebüro	rye-zer-boo-roe
department store	Warenhaus	vahr'n-hows
hairdresser	Friseur	freezz-er
newspaper kiosk	Zeitungskiosk	tsytoongs-kee-osk
bookshop	Buchhandlung	bookh-hant-loong
bakery	Bäckerei	beck-er-eye
post office	Post	posst
shop/store	Geschäft/Laden	gush-eft/lard'n
shoe shop	Schuhladen	shoo-lard'n
clothes shop	Kleiderladen, Boutique	klyder-lard'n boo-teek-uh
food shop	Lebensmittel-geschäft	lay-bens-mittel-gush-eft

Staying in a Hotel

Do you have any vacancies?	**Haben Sie noch Zimmer frei?**	harb'n zee nokh tsimm-er-fry
with twin beds?	**mit zwei Betten?**	mitt tsvy bett'n
with a double bed?	**mit einem Doppelbett?**	mitt ine'm dopp'l-bet
with a bath?	**mit Bad?**	mitt hart
with a shower?	**mit Dusche?**	mitt doosh-uh
I have a reservation	**Ich habe eine Reservierung**	ish harb-uh ine-uh rez-er-veer-oong
key	**Schlüssel**	shlooss'l
porter	**Pförtner**	pfert-ner

Eating Out

Do you have a table for…?	**Haben Sie einen Tisch für…?**	harb'n zee ine-uhn tish foor
I would like to reserve a table	**Ich möchte eine Reservierung machen**	ish mer-shtuh ine-uh rezer-veer-oong-makh'n
Waiter!	**Herr Ober!**	hair oh-bare!
The bill (check)	**Die Rechnung**	dee resh-noong
breakfast	**Frühstück**	froo-shtock
lunch	**Mittagessen**	mit-targ-ess'n
dinner	**Abendessen**	arb'nt-ess'n
bottle	**Flasche**	flush-uh
dish of the day	**Tagesgericht**	tahg-es-gur-isht
main dish	**Hauptgericht**	howpt-gur-isht
dessert	**Nachtisch**	nahkh-tish
cup	**Tasse**	tass-uh
wine list	**Weinkarte**	vine-kart-uh
glass	**Glas**	glars
spoon	**Löffel**	lerff'l
tip	**Trinkgeld**	trink-gelt
knife	**Messer**	mess-er
starter (appetizer)	**Vorspeise**	for-shpize-uh
plate	**Teller**	tell-er
fork	**Gabel**	gahb'l

Menu Decoder

Beefsteak	**beef**-stayk	steak
Bier	beer	beer
Branntwein	brant-vine	spirits
Bratkartoffeln	brat-kar-toff'ln	fried potatoes
Bratwurst	brat-voorst	fried sausage
Brötchen	bret-tchen	bread roll
Brot	brot	bread
Brühe	bruh-uh	broth
Butter	boot-ter	butter
Champignon	shum-pin-yong	mushroom
Ei	eye	egg
Eis	ice	ice/ice cream
Ente	ent-uh	duck
Fisch	fish	fish
Forelle	for-ell-uh	trout
Frikadelle	Frika-dayl-uh	hamburger
Gans	ganns	goose
Garnele	gar-nayl-uh	prawn/shrimp
gebraten	g'braat'n	fried
gegrillt	g'grilt	grilled
gekocht	g'kokht	boiled
geräuchert	g'rowk-ert	smoked
Gemüse	g'mooz-uh	vegetables
Hähnchen	haynsh'n	chicken
Kaffee	kaf-fay	coffee
Kalbfleisch	kalp-flysh	veal
Karpfen	karpf'n	carp
Käse	kayz-uh	cheese
Knoblauch	k'nob-lowkh	garlic
Knödel	k'nerd'l	noodle
Kohl	koal	cabbage
Kuchen	kookh'n	cake
Milch	milsh	milk
Mineralwasser	minn-er-arl-vuss-er	mineral water
Öl	erl	oil
Pfeffer	pfeff-er	pepper
Rindfleisch	rint-flysh	beef
Saft	zuft	juice
Salat	zal-aat	salad
Salz	zults	salt
Salzkartoffeln	zults-kar-toff'l	boiled potatoes
Sekt	zekt	sparkling wine
scharf	sharf	spicy
Schnitzel	shnitz'l	veal/pork cutlet
Schweinefleisch	shvine-flysh	pork
Spargel	shparg'l	asparagus
Spinat	shpin-art	spinach
Tee	tay	tea
Wein	vine	wine
Wiener Würstchen	veen-er voorst-sh'n	frankfurter
Zucker	tsook-er	sugar
Zwiebel	tsveeb'l	onion

Numbers

0	null	nool
1	eins	eye'ns
2	zwei	tsvy
3	drei	dry
4	vier	feer
5	fünf	foonf
6	sechs	zex
7	sieben	zeeb'n
8	acht	uhkht
9	neun	noyn
10	zehn	tsayn
11	elf	elf
12	zwölf	tserlf
13	dreizehn	dry-tsayn
14	vierzehn	feer-tsayn
15	fünfzehn	foonf-tsayn
16	sechzehn	zex-tsayn
17	siebzehn	zeep-tsayn
18	achtzehn	uhkht-tsayn
19	neunzehn	noyn-tsayn
20	zwanzig	tsvunn-tsig
21	einundzwanzig	ine-oont-tsvunn-tsig
30	dreissig	dry-sig
40	vierzig	feer-sig
50	fünfzig	foonf-tsig
60	sechzig	zex-tsig
70	siebzig	zeep-tsig
80	achtzig	uhkht-tsig
90	neunzig	noyn-tsig
100	hundert	hoond't
1000	tausend	towz'nt
1,000,000	eine Million	ine-uh mill-yon

Time

one minute	**eine Minute**	ine-uh min-oot-uh
one hour	**eine Stunde**	ine-uh shtoond-uh
Monday	**Montag**	mohn-targ
Tuesday	**Dienstag**	deens-targ
Wednesday	**Mittwoch**	mitt-vokh
Thursday	**Donnerstag**	donn-ers-targ
Friday	**Freitag**	fry-targ
Saturday	**Samstag**	zums-targ
Sunday	**Sonntag**	zon-targ

Selected Street Index